Sport Policy Across the United Kingdom

This book provides a comparative analysis of sport and physical activity policies, processes, and practices across the home nations (England, Scotland, Wales, and Northern Ireland) of the United Kingdom.

Drawing upon in-depth analysis by internationally recognised experts within the sport policy and management field, and applying a novel analytical framework, this book offers the first comprehensive intra-country comparison of the most significant features of the sporting infrastructure across the home nations. With chapters focusing on each of the four nations in detail, followed by a comparative chapter that identifies themes regarding the evolution of sport policy across the UK, the book examines the differences and similarities across elite, community, and school sport policy. It provides an important insight into how sport policy interacts with national and devolved political structures and with sociocultural factors to drive both elite sporting success and community sport development.

This book is essential reading for any student, researcher, policymaker or sport practitioner with an interest in sport policy, sport development, sport management, public policy, or politics.

Mathew Dowling is Senior Lecturer in the Cambridge Centre for Sport and Exercise Sciences at Anglia Ruskin University, UK. His current research interests focus on the application of organisational and political theory to understand sport organisations and systems. He has published widely in sport policy and politics, organisational change, governance, professionalisation, and comparative methods in sport.

Spencer Harris is Associate Professor of Sport Management at the University of Colorado, Colorado Springs, USA. He has more than 30 years' experience within the sport development industry and has worked for the University of Hertfordshire, Sport England, and Right to Play. His research interests centre on sport governance, sport policy, and the sport-politics relationship.

Chris Mackintosh is Senior Lecturer of Sport Development in the Department for Sport and Exercise Sciences at The Manchester Institute of Sport, Manchester Metropolitan University, UK. In 2020–2021 he was appointed the special policy advisor to the House of Lords Special Inquiry into a National Plan for Sport and Recreation, which was debated in UK Parliament in February 2023. He is Chair and Founder of the United Kingdom Sport Development Network (UKSDN). His current research interests include public policy of sport development and delivering systems in national governing bodies, local government, and the role of the voluntary sector.

Routledge Focus on Sport, Culture and Society

Routledge Focus on Sport, Culture and Society showcases the latest cutting-edge research in the sociology of sport and exercise. Concise in form (20,000-50,000 words) and published quickly (within three months), the books in this series represents an important channel through which authors can disseminate their research swiftly and make an impact on current debates. We welcome submissions on any topic within the socio-cultural study of sport and exercise, including but not limited to subjects such as gender, race, sexuality, disability, politics, the media, social theory, Olympic Studies, and the ethics and philosophy of sport. The series aims to be theoretically-informed, empirically-grounded and international in reach, and will include a diversity of methodological approaches.

Available in this series:

On Boxing
Critical Interventions in the Bittersweet Science
Joseph D Lewandowski

Sport, Forced Migration and the 'Refugee Crisis'
Enrico Michelini

Sport Policy Across the United Kingdom
A Comparative Analysis
Edited by Mathew Dowling, Spencer Harris, and Chris Mackintosh

For more information about this series, please visit: https://www.routledge.com/Routledge-Focus-on-Sport-Culture-and-Society/book-series/RFSCS

Sport Policy Across the United Kingdom

A Comparative Analysis

**Edited by
Mathew Dowling, Spencer Harris, and
Chris Mackintosh**

LONDON AND NEW YORK

First published 2023
by Routledge
4 Park Square, Milton Park, Abingdon, Oxon OX14 4RN

and by Routledge
605 Third Avenue, New York, NY 10158

Routledge is an imprint of the Taylor & Francis Group, an informa business

© 2023 selection and editorial matter, Mathew Dowling, Spencer Harris, and Chris Mackintosh; individual chapters, the contributors

The right of Mathew Dowling, Spencer Harris, and Chris Mackintosh to be identified as the authors of the editorial material, and of the authors for their individual chapters, has been asserted in accordance with sections 77 and 78 of the Copyright, Designs and Patents Act 1988.

All rights reserved. No part of this book may be reprinted or reproduced or utilised in any form or by any electronic, mechanical, or other means, now known or hereafter invented, including photocopying and recording, or in any information storage or retrieval system, without permission in writing from the publishers.

Trademark notice: Product or corporate names may be trademarks or registered trademarks, and are used only for identification and explanation without intent to infringe.

British Library Cataloguing-in-Publication Data
A catalogue record for this book is available from the British Library

Library of Congress Cataloging-in-Publication Data
Names: Dowling, Mathew, editor. | Harris, Spencer, editor. | Mackintosh, Chris, editor.
Title: Sport policy Across the United Kingdom : a comparative analysis / edited by Mathew Dowling, Spencer Harris and Chris Mackintosh.
Description: New York : Routledge, 2023. | Series: Routledge focus on sport, culture and society | Includes bibliographical references and index. |
Identifiers: LCCN 2022060767 | ISBN 9781032148083 (Hardback) | ISBN 9781032148113 (Paperback) | ISBN 9781003241232 (eBook)
Subjects: LCSH: Sports and state—England. | Sports and state—Scotland. | Sports and state—Wales. | Sports and state—Northern Ireland.
Classification: LCC GV706.35 .S65 2023 | DDC 796.0942—dc23/eng/20230109
LC record available at https://lccn.loc.gov/2022060767

ISBN: 978-1-032-14808-3 (hbk)
ISBN: 978-1-032-14811-3 (pbk)
ISBN: 978-1-003-24123-2 (ebk)

DOI: 10.4324/9781003241232

Typeset in Times New Roman
by codeMantra

To Mum
  – Mathew Dowling
To Mona, Maya, and Arlo
  – Spencer Harris
To Simon
  – Chris Mackintosh

Contents

List of figures xi
List of tables xiii
List of abbreviations xv
List of contributors xvii

1 **Introduction** 1
   MATHEW DOWLING, SPENCER HARRIS, AND
   CHRIS MACKINTOSH

2 **Sport Policy in England** 20
   IAIN LINDSEY AND DANIEL BLOYCE

3 **Sport Policy in Scotland** 40
   GRANT JARVIE

4 **Sport Policy in Wales** 60
   NICOLA BOLTON

5 **Sport Policy in Northern Ireland** 83
   KYLE FERGUSON, PAUL DONNELLY,
   ROBERT HEYBURN, AND SIMON SHIBLI

6 **Conclusion** 108
   MATHEW DOWLING, SPENCER HARRIS, AND
   CHRIS MACKINTOSH

Appendix 1	Sport policy Across the United Kingdom: A comparative analysis	129
Appendix 2	Sport Policy Across the United Kingdom (SPATUK) – Systematic Review	147
Index		149

Figures

1.1	Embedded case study design to examine sport policy across the United Kingdom	12
4.1	Sport Wales's Active Young People Programmes	72
5.1	The structure of sport in the United Kingdom and Republic of Ireland	84
5.2	Sport and physical activity continuum	90
5.3	Northern Ireland's performance in the Commonwealth Games 1998–2022	93
5.4	Foundation blocks for the *Active Living Strategy*	95
5.5	Participation rates in the most popular sports and activities in Northern Ireland – adults (16+ years)	96

Tables

1.1	Key Stakeholders in Delivering Sport Participation and High-Performance Sport within Home Nations	8
1.2	Analytical Framework	15
4.1	Strategy and Policy Impacting on the Development of Sport in Wales (1997–2022)	63
4.2	The Well-Being of Future Generations (Wales) Act 2015	66
5.1	The Components of the Talent Framework Adopted by Sport NI	93
5.2	Community Sport Participation for Primary and Post-Primary School Pupils	97
5.3	Most Popular Community Sports for Primary and Post-Primary School Pupils Combined over the Last 12 Months	98

Abbreviations

ALS	Active Lives Survey
APs	Active Partnerships
APS	Active People Survey
AYPP	Active Young People Programmes
BAME	Black, Asian, and Minority Ethnic
BOA	British Olympic Association
CCEA	Council for the Curriculum, Examinations and Assessment
CCPR	Central Council for Physical Recreation
CHS	Continuous Household Survey
CMO	Chief Medical Officer
COSLA	Convention of Scottish Local Authorities
CSP	County Sport Partnerships/Curriculum Sports Programme
CSPPA	Children's Sport Participation and Physical Activity
DCMS	Department of Digital, Culture, Media and Sport
DE	Department for/of Education
DfC	Department for Communities
DfE	Department for Education/Department for Economy
DNH	Department of National Heritage
EIS	English Institute of Sport
EU	European Union
GAA	Gaelic Athletic Association
GB	Great Britain
GLFW	Governance and Leadership Framework for Wales
HAF	Healthy and Active Fund
HEIs	Higher Education Institutions
IFA	Irish Football Association
INGBs	Irish National Governing Bodies
LAs	Local Authorities

xvi *Abbreviations*

LISPA	Lifelong Involvement in Sport and Physical Activity
MDSD	Most Different Systems Design
MP	Member of Parliament
MSP	Member of Scottish Parliament
MSSD	Most Similar Systems Design
NCPE	National Curriculum for Physical Education
NDPB	Non-departmental public body
NGB	National Governing Bodies of Sport
NGOs	National governing organisations
NI	Northern Ireland
NICWGC	Northern Ireland Commonwealth Games Council
NINGBs	Northern Ireland National Governing Bodies of Sport
NISF	Northern Ireland Sports Forum
NRW	National Resources Wales
OCI	Olympic Council of Ireland
ONS	Office for National Statistics
PCI	Paralympic Council of Ireland
PE	physical education
PESS	Physical Education and School Sport
PfG	Programme for Government
PHW	Public Health Wales
PLPS	Physical Literacy Programme for Schools
ROI	Republic of Ireland
SDG	Sustainable Development Goals
SINI	Sports Institute Northern Ireland
SNI	Sport Northern Ireland
SNISI	Sport Northern Ireland Sport Institute
SNP	Scottish National Party
SSPs	School Sport Partnerships
T:BUC	Together: Building a United Community
UK	United Kingdom
UNCRC	United Nations Convention on the Rights of Child
USA	United States of America
WBFGA	Well-being of Future Generations Act
WHO	World Health Organisation
WSPs	Whole Sport Plans

Contributors

Daniel Bloyce is Professor of the Sociology of Sport at the University of Chester, UK. He was a co-founder (with Professors Barrie Houlihan and Andy Smith) of the *International Journal of Sport Policy and Politics*.

Nicola Bolton is Professor of Strategic Policy and Practice at Cardiff Metropolitan University and Head of Department in the Cardiff School of Management, UK. Her research interests focus on sport policy, strategy, and governance, and include various evaluations of national sport and physical activity interventions. Previously, Nicola worked as a senior executive in public policy. She has served on the boards of British Gymnastics (2013–2022), the British Gymnastics Foundation (2014–2021), and Sport Wales (2004–2007).

Paul Donnelly is Lecturer in Sports Development and Coaching at Ulster University, Belfast, Northern Ireland. Previously, Paul was the Regeneration Director with the Gaelic Athletic Association (2018–2021) and Head of Policy, Planning and Research at Sport Northern Ireland (2002–2018).

Kyle Ferguson is Reader in Coach Education and Management at Ulster University, Belfast, Northern Ireland. Kyle has led a range of national and international research programmes in sport and physical activity focusing on cohesion and measurement. At a policy level, Kyle is a board member of Sport Northern Ireland overseeing the promotion of sport.

Robert Heyburn is Senior Policy Development Manager in the Department for Communities, Belfast, Northern Ireland. He led the development and implementation of the 2009–2019 Sport Matters Strategy, the Active Living: No Limits Action Plan 2016–2021 for those living with disabilities, and the Wellbeing in Sport Action

Plan 2019–2025 supporting mental health and well-being for all. In 2015, he led a review of Sport Matters and latterly brought forward the new Active Living NI Strategy for Sport and Physical Activity.

Grant Jarvie is Professor and Chair of Sport at the University of Edinburgh, UK, and has held leadership positions within both higher education and the sports industry including Acting University Principal and Director with the board of *sportscotland*. He is a visiting professor in the University of Toronto, Canada, and serves on the board of several football clubs.

Iain Lindsey is Associate Professor of Sport Policy and Development in the Department of Sport and Exercise Sciences at Durham University, UK. He has published widely on youth and community sport policy, across the United Kingdom and international contexts.

Simon Shibli is Professor of Sport Management and Director of the Sport Industry Research Centre (SIRC) at Sheffield Hallam University, UK. His main research interests are in the applied use of techniques from the fields of finance and economics to research questions in sport and leisure.

1 Introduction

Mathew Dowling, Spencer Harris, and Chris Mackintosh

The United Kingdom (UK) has a long and complicated history encompassing a series of unions (and separations) between England, Scotland, Wales, and Ireland (and later Northern Ireland). Governments, public schools, and civic society have all played an important role in the evolution of sport across the UK. We see examples of this in the sport-related statues that date back as far as the medieval and Tudor periods (Brailsford, 1991), in the disputes – between parliamentarians and monarchs – about when sports should be played (Dougall, 2011), and in the efforts of governments to exercise their power to maintain class privileges in relation to sport, specifically in relation to the preservation of fox and stag hunting and in the banning of working-class sports such as bull- and bear-baiting (Houlihan, 1997). In the 20th century, a high-minded civil society was pivotal in creating mass sporting events (e.g., the Much Wenlock Games), embracing sport within the philosophy and curricula of public schools, and providing opportunities to play sport through the sheer growth in the voluntary sport clubs and associations across the country (Holt, 1990). Over more recent years, developments reveal a growing government interest in sport, where sport can be seen to represent a key part of the government's domestic social welfare programme and its overseas diplomacy efforts.

Despite these developments, the literature remains sparse in the attention given to sport policy across the UK, particularly the distinctiveness and similarities in sport policy processes and practices across the four home nations that make up the UK. Instead, it is far more common for researchers (including our own previous work) to supplant the UK with a focus on policy developments across England. This is most commonly due to word count limitations and the significant difference in the amount of work required in analysing policy across one nation (England) as opposed to addressing policy across five nations (i.e., specific policy in each of the four home nations plus

DOI: 10.4324/9781003241232-1

UK-wide policy). Ultimately, it is this gap in the literature—the lack of attention to specific policy in England, Scotland, Wales, and Northern Ireland as individual home countries and also as part of UK-wide policy—that drives our interest in publishing this book. In so doing, *we aim to provide an intra-country comparative analysis of sport and physical activity policy, processes, and practice across the home nations of the United Kingdom.*

From the outset, we believe it is important to discuss and clarify the key terms used throughout the book. As indicated above, when referring to the UK, we mean the United Kingdom of Great Britain (which is made up of England, Scotland, Wales, and Northern Ireland). These four nations are commonly referred to as home nations or home countries. This distinction is particularly evident in international sporting competition whereby home nations combine efforts to compete as 'Team GB' at the Olympic and Paralympic Games but then compete as separate countries in certain national sporting contests (football, rugby) and in multi-sport events such as the Commonwealth Games. It is for this reason that we have used the terms home nations and home countries interchangeably, allowing the country authors to use their preferred choice of language when referring to their own country context.

Conceptually, the policy process has been presented as a series of stages involving problems, agenda setting, policy options, decision-making, implementation, and evaluation (De Leon, 1999). While we accept the temptation to apply such practical stages to the analysis of policy, we agree that such approaches are neo-positivist and overly rationale, and reflect an uncritical assumption of the separation of fact from value (Houlihan, 2005). Consequently, we adopt a broader and nuanced conceptualisation of the policy process where the policy environment consists of interacting elements such as institutions, rules, actors, networks, ideas and beliefs, policy conditions (economic, social, demographic), and the key focusing events that influence policy choices (Cairney, 2019).

As a discrete policy sector, sport policy can be seen to represent the ideas and interests of government, national sport organisations, and other key stakeholders, and outline the direction that sport should take (Byers et al., 2012). It is "characterised by recency, increasing government intervention, embedded beliefs, a dispersed administrative context, and experiences of significant exogenous influences" (Hoekman & Scheerder, 2021, p. 105). Sport policy goals are commonly focused on achieving distinct sporting outcomes (e.g., increases in mass participation, athlete development, coach development, club development, enhanced performance in international competitions) and/or social outcomes (e.g., physical and mental well-being, individual development, community development, economic development). In our references to the comparative analysis of policy, we are particularly concerned with questions concerning the relationship between sport policy and the differing political systems, policy processes, and policy outputs and outcomes across the four home countries. Comparative analysis of this type—particularly in the context of the UK and the home nations—can reveal culturally bound generalisations and assumptions about specific policy concerns and enhance our insights into the specificity of sport policy across the UK. It can also enable cross-nation learning and exchange to strengthen collaboration in the UK sport policy process and maintain the uniqueness and specificity of the home country sport policy process.

The following sections in this chapter address the peculiarities of the UK context, provide a brief overview of how sport is organised in the UK, and set out the methodological approach and analytical framework used to guide the development of each chapter. We conclude with a summary of the key points and a brief outline of the structure of the book.

Exploring the United Kingdom: unification, devolution, and independence

While the UK remains a sovereign nation, the union of the four home countries has been consistently challenged and—in the post-Brexit reality of 2023—remains as contentious as ever. The union has a long history with its formal arrangements dating back to the 16th century when the UK was reduced to two nations—the Kingdom of England (which included Wales and controlled Ireland) and the Kingdom of Scotland. In 1603, the Union of the Crowns saw James VI of Scotland ascending to the throne as James I of the Kingdom of England. While the unification of two states under one monarch did result in some unified decisions, the Crown of Scotland and the Crown of England largely remained separate and distinct (Galloway, 1986). This all changed in the 18th and 19th centuries through the enactment of the respective Acts of Union between England and Scotland (1707) and Great Britain and Ireland (1801). In 1922, the Irish Free State withdrew from the Union with the six counties[1] of Northern Ireland, the remaining part of what is today known as the United Kingdom of Great Britain and Northern Ireland.

The series of unifications that led to the creation of the United Kingdom of Great Britain and Northern Ireland were politically expedient—not only in the case of the Great Britain–Ireland union, which galvanised a broader, collective response to the war with France, but also in addressing important economic and social reforms. However, the extent to which these reforms have been realised across the UK is contested (Stafford, 2022). Additionally, the Acts may be seen to be problematic insofar as they address the unification of the four home nations without attending to the practical problems of land, religion, and politics, not to mention the ongoing tension of power and influence, particularly on key decisions concerning governance, representation, the democratic process, the redistribution of wealth, and autonomy.

Towards the end of the 1990s, in response to the rise of nationalism in Wales and Scotland, the ongoing conflict in Northern Ireland, demands for proportional representation, and calls for the autonomous governance of home nations, the UK government devolved executive power to Wales, Scotland, and Northern Ireland and decentralised power across the eight regions of England. Following referenda in each home country (Scotland and Wales in 1997; Northern Ireland in 1999), new devolved legislatures and executives were introduced in May 1999. Over the past 20 years, the devolved institutions across the home countries[2] have structurally evolved, assuming wider responsibilities and greater powers (HM Government, 2019), including the development of domestic sport policy through each parliament/assembly and the coordination on of UK-wide sport policy through the UK Parliament. There is no elected English parliament, and while there were plans to create elected regional assemblies across England, these plans were abandoned in 2004 due to a lack of voter support. Consequently, decision-making in England remains centralised with power concentrated in the UK Parliament. In 2015, the English votes for English laws system was introduced, requiring that laws passed in the UK Parliament that only apply to England must have the support of the majority of Parliamentarians from English constituencies.

These developments together with the strengthening sense of distinctiveness of Scotland and Wales, and to a lesser extent Northern Ireland, reinforces arguments about the decline of Britishness and the collapse of the union (Nairn, 2000). Some Conservative commentators argue that devolution is—along with other issues such as the European Union, immigration, and a broad-based multi-culturalism—the very reason why Britain is in decline (Hitchen, 2008). Adding to this, Gilroy (2004) points to the obsessive focus on invasion, war, and a loss of identity fed by technology, deindustrialisation, consumerism, loneliness, and a fracturing of family forms that have forever changed British culture. Threats to the continuation of the union are most visible in Scotland. In 2014, the Scottish government organised a referendum on independence with an exceptionally high turnout (84.6%) but with the majority of voters (55.3%) rejecting Scottish independence (HM Government, 2014). Prior to the 2016 Scottish Parliament election, the pro-independence Scottish National Party stated that it would hold a second referendum if there was a material change of circumstances since the 2014 referendum, specifying that the UK vote to leave the European Union represented such a change (Scottish National Party, 2016). As the UK moved closer to leaving the EU, the SNP leader gained approval from the Scottish Parliament to organise a second referendum (The Scottish Parliament, 2017). At the time of writing, the status of such a referendum remains unclear largely due to a constitutional stand-off. The Scottish National Party wants to pass a Scottish bill to allow the referendum to go ahead, but the UK government believe that the future of the union is reserved to Westminster, and thus, the Scottish Parliament cannot legislate for an independence referendum without straying beyond their devolved powers (Sim, 2021).

While Brexit is undoubtedly an important exogenous factor influencing the Scottish National Party's stance, their latest position reinforces the classic nationalist view where Scotland has a duty and right to govern its own affairs—in their entirety—rather than those issues to which the UK Parliament has reached agreement. Another important part of the argument for independence lays in basic economics, that is, the belief that Scotland could do better alone as a small European country—giving it complete independence, control of spending, and direct oversight of its natural resources (Macfarlane, 2021). Additionally, Scotland's pursuit of independence is also related to identity. Here, Britain—a multinational, democratic state—reflects the overwhelming political, social, and cultural dominance of England in a similar way to how the Swiss-Germans dominate the Swiss federation or the Anglo-Canadians the Canadian federation (Kumar, 2010). Britain and Britishness are strongly connected to the Crown, the UK Parliament, the Protestant religion, and the worldwide British empire (Kumar, 2000). The same does not hold for many across Scotland. Moreover, Brexit represents a line in the sand, a divergence of attitudes in Scotland and the UK on the question of European Union membership, with the vote to leave demonstrating how Scotland is being ignored (Macfarlane, 2021). Importantly, in years gone by, pro-independence, pro-Europe, and support for the Scottish National Party all represented different and separate ideas, whereas today they have merged (Keating, 2019). While, at the time of writing, the union remains, it is clear that Brexit and the sovereignty of the people over the sovereignty of the UK Parliament pose significant threats to the continuation of the union and its post-Brexit survival.

Sport in the United Kingdom

Historically, sport has played an important role in building distinct values and identities of each home nation. For the Catholic northern Irish, the restoration of the Gaelic games provided an ideal tool to express its cultural distinctiveness and separation from England. For the Southern Welsh valleys, rugby provided a particular brand of sport to capture the enthusiasm of the bustling coal mine and metalworker industry (Holt, 1990). For Scotland, identity among the masses was embedded in association football and their deep and bitter rivalry with England. For Victorian England, cricket proved an ideal symbol to demonstrate the ostensible import of values such as respectability, morality, and the good graces of the gentleman amateur. While it is true that this historic sporting nationalism influences sport in the home nations to this day, it is also true that globalisation, commercialisation, and governmentalisation have reshaped the UK sporting landscape, resulting in an increasingly homogenous diet of sports dominated by large, commercial sports such as football and rugby union.

As will become apparent, sport policy and sporting structures in the UK reflect the need to balance the implications of devolution with the requirements to retain UK representation in almost all international sport competitions.[3] Consequently, sport policy and sporting structures within the UK operate on two interconnected levels. The policies and structures for physical education, school sport, and community sport are overseen by the devolved power for each home nation, whereas elite sport policy and structures are developed and overseen at the UK level. In Scotland, school and community sport policy is devolved to the Scottish Parliament and administered by the Scottish Executive with strategic and operational support from Sport Scotland. Similar arrangements follow in Northern Ireland through its National Assembly and with support provided by Sport Northern Ireland. Wales has a devolved government (Welsh Government/*Llywodraeth Cymru*) with oversight over Sport Wales (*Chwaraeon Cymru*) which advises the Welsh Government on sporting matters. In England, the Department for Digital, Culture, Media and Sport (DCMS) works in collaboration with other government departments (health, education, local government) to oversee school and community sport policy and implement this nationally through Sport England. Elite sport policy and structures are overseen by the DCMS in collaboration with UK Sport and the respective UK and/or home country National Governing Body of Sport.[4] A more detailed discussion and analysis of home country sport policy, structures, and strategy is provided in the following chapters.

Pilot study – Sport Policy Across the United Kingdom (SPATUK)

The initial idea for this book stemmed from a small-scale pilot study that we undertook to explore the current state of sport and physical activity sport policies and processes across the UK. The pilot project entitled 'Sport Policy Across the United Kingdom' (SPATUK) was designed to identify how sport is organised and structured within each home nation as well as identify some emerging themes surrounding the similarities and differences of sport policy processes and practices within each of the home nations (England, Scotland, Wales, and Northern Ireland). The project was coordinated by Dr Mathew Dowling (Anglia Ruskin University), Dr Spencer Harris (University of Colorado), and Dr Chris Mackintosh (Manchester Metropolitan University) (co-principal investigators) and supported by research assistants (postgraduate students) and our contributors. The project involved a short online questionnaire (see Appendix 1) designed to produce descriptive statistics and key themes. Participants were recruited based on convenience and snowballing sampling technique and utilising the research teams' own professional networks. A small, targeted group of 23 participants completed the online survey. Whilst we recognise that this is not sufficient to make any definitive claims about the nature and extent of sport policies across the UK, it did nonetheless provide interesting insights into, and by extension offered further support for, the need to examine the current state of sport policies across the home nations. Many studies to date have primarily focused their analysis within each of the home nations including England (e.g., Harris et al., 2009; Mackintosh, 2011; Mackintosh & Liddle, 2015, Thompson et al., 2021), Wales (e.g., McInch & Fleming, 2022), Northern Ireland (e.g., Bairner, 2004; Hassan & Telford, 2014), and Scotland (e.g., Jarvie & Reid, 1999; Reid, 2009, 2012). This exploratory pilot study was therefore a useful starting point for conducting this larger comparative study, which is the first of its kind to systematically compare sport policies across all four home nations.

Of particular note, respondents described the sport and physical activity system within their home nation as 'complex', 'confusing', and 'under-resourced'. Some respondents went so far as to describe it as 'fractured', 'disparate', and even 'in decline'. Similar choices of language are also conveyed by the contributors of this book in the chapters that follow. As part of the survey, we also asked respondents to identify who they considered to be key stakeholders responsible for delivering (1) sport and physical activity participation and (2) high-performance sport objectives. This list is outlined verbatim in Table 1.1.

Table 1.1 Key Stakeholders in Delivering Sport Participation and High-Performance Sport within Home Nations

Key Stakeholders – Sport Participation	Key Stakeholders – High-Performance Sport
Government	UK Sport
Sport England	Government
Local government	Higher Education
Public Health England	National Governing Bodies
Active Partnerships	Sport Clubs
Schools	Sport England
Further Education providers	British Olympic Association
Higher Education providers	English Institute of Sport
Local Authorities	Private/Commercial Organisations
Private Leisure operators	Universities
Public health teams	Professional sport clubs
Highway agencies	National Lottery
Town and planning departments	Active Partnerships
Property developers	Lobbying Groups
Parish councils	Athletes
Playing Field Associations	International Sport Organisations
Community Centres	Commonwealth Games Federation
UK Active	Department of Digital, Culture, Media, and Sport
Sport and Recreation Alliance	
Sports Clubs	
Youth Sport Trust	
Health and social care services	
Media and broadcasters	
Activity Alliance	
Women in Sport	
Mass event providers	
Third sector/charities	
Association for Physical Education	

Introduction 9

Two observations can be made from the list of stakeholders identified in Table 1.1. First, the respondents often adopted a 'top-down' perspective on the delivery of sport participation and high performance. In this sense, respondents tended to identify the most visible, often national-level organisations. Second, and linked to this point, is the fact that there was no general agreement, particularly in relation to sport participation and physical activity, regarding who is responsible for delivering these objectives both within home nations and across the UK. This finding was also supported by the fact that nearly three-quarters of the respondents (71.4%) either disagreed or strongly disagreed that roles and responsibilities of key stakeholders within sport and physical activity are clearly defined. Similarly, over half of the respondents (61.9%) disagreed or strongly disagreed that their home nation's sporting landscape is a coordinated system.

We also asked a series of questions relating to the coordination and communication and found that:

- 90.4% strongly agreed or agreed that coordination for planning and delivery of sport and physical activity could be improved within their home nation;
- 76.2% strongly agreed or agreed that coordination for planning and delivery of sport and physical activity could be improved within the UK;
- 95.2% strongly agreed or agreed that communication for planning and delivery of sport and physical activity could be improved within their home nation;
- 90.5% strongly agreed or agreed that communication for planning and delivery of sport and physical activity could be improved within the UK.

Interestingly, when asked whether sport and physical activity policy across the UK has historically been England-centric, 38.1% of respondents neither agreed or disagreed, 42.9% agreed or strongly agreed, and 19% disagreed. However, these findings emanate from a survey with a strong England-centric sample bias. There was also a mixed response to whether current sport and physical activity policy across the UK was England-centric: 38.1% neither agreed or disagreed, 38.1% agreed or strongly agreed, and 23.8% disagreed. Taken collectively, these responses suggest, based on our sample, there are mixed views regarding whether sport policy has been, or is currently, England-centric.

Although we recognise the limitations of this pilot study, including the limited sample size and the England-centric sample bias (17/23), the findings reveal the inherent complexities and intricacies that exist within the planning and delivery of sport policy in the UK in general and the home nations specifically, and it also provides additional support for the need for further study examining the relationships and interconnectedness between home nations. The next two sections outline our methodological approach and analytical framework for the present study.

Comparing home nations – methodological approach

To conduct an intra-country comparative analysis of sport and physical activity policies, processes, and practices across the UK, we adopted a comparative approach utilising a case-based research design. Regarding the former, our choice of wording of comparative 'approach' rather than 'method' is deliberate in that we inherently recognise that our book represents a compilation of four in-depth, holistic cases (Yin, 2017) addressing sport policies, processes, and practices within England, Scotland, Wales, and Northern Ireland. We adopt the term comparative in its broadest sense to refer to a general research strategy (or approach) rather than a specific data collection technique that can be directly contrasted to experimental or statistical methods (Lijphart, 1971).

Our methodological approach is comparative for several reasons. First, our interest and emphasis in collecting these in-depth accounts of the four home nations is to generate broader inferences about the nature and extent of sport policy across the UK. Rather than just focusing on interesting and unique features of each case, whilst interesting it itself, our primary focus is on utilising these detailed accounts to understand the similarities and differences that may or may not exist between cases. Our approach represents an embedded, multi-case design, with four embedded cases that contribute to a broader examination of the UK. See below for further elaboration of the sample.

Second, the editors created, and the contributors adopted, a singular analytical framework *a priori* to support a comparative analysis. The adoption of a singular analytical framework provided us (i.e., editors and contributors) with a useful starting point and structuring device to examine each individual case in a like-for-like manner. It also enabled us to begin to identify broader inferences and general patterns regarding the similarities and differences that exist between home nations. In other words, the adoption of a comparative methodological approach provides us with a useful starting point, enabling us to move beyond description to more theoretically informed accounts of sport policies, processes, and practices (Landman & Carvalho, 2017). We outline our analytical framework in more detail below.

Third, we inherently recognise – as other comparative methodologists (Dogan & Pelassy, 1990; Landman & Carvalho, 2017; Lijphart, 1971; Øyen, 1990; Sartori, 1970; Schuster, 2007) and sport scholars (Dowling et al., 2018; Dowling & Harris, 2021) have done elsewhere – the series of philosophical, methodological, and practical challenges of comparative research that should be considered when making comparisons. Whilst we have done our best to highlight the limitations of our study (see below), we accept the methodological and practical trade-offs that are inherent in studies of this nature. We therefore adopt a *comparativist* approach insofar as we acknowledge the limitations of comparative analysis but argue that it can only be advanced through further questioning of its distinctiveness and that comparative analysis more accurately constitutes an 'imperfect' art and science (Øyen, 1990). Consequently, we adopt a similar approach to Jowell (1998), who cautions that comparative researchers should be as enthusiastic about their limitations as they are about their findings.

Comparing home nations: adopting a case-based approach

The decision to focus specifically on the sport policies across the UK makes the selection of cases a self-selecting process. We adopted a 'small-N' approach with a set of purposefully selected cases (England, Scotland, Wales, and Northern Ireland), based on geopolitical and constitutional boundaries. The emphasis of our case-oriented (Ragin, 2014) or case-based (Della Porta, 2008) approach is to understand the complexities of social phenomenon through an in-depth, intensive examination of each case to be able to compare the similarities and differences between them (Ragin, 2014). Due to the predetermined selection of cases, our study does not strictly adhere to either a *most similar systems design* or a *most different system design* (MSSD/MDSD) (Ancker, 2008). Nonetheless, our study more closely aligned with a *most similar system design* with countries being as similar as possible in order to allow for meaningful comparisons to be made (Landman & Carvalho, 2017). The selection of similar or 'like-for-like' cases assumes that certain features (e.g., political, welfare systems, socio-demographics) of a case are similar across each case with differences being attributed to the uniqueness of each case. As highlighted

12 *Mathew Dowling et al.*

above, we recognise that there are notable similarities with regard to the key features within our sample, which in our view, make an intra-country comparison of this kind particularly fertile as it is possible to identify explanatory factors more precisely. In support of this viewpoint, Przeworski and Teune (1970) argue that "systems as similar as possible with respect to as many features as possible constitute the optimal samples for comparative inquiry" (p. 32). Consistent with the MSSD sampling approach, we adopted a multiple, embedded, case study design (see Figure 1.1).

In developing our sample, we were mindful that "comparability is not inherent in any given area, but is more likely within an area than a randomly selected set of countries" (Lijphart, 1971, p. 689). Thus, whilst we adopted an area- or geographical-based study, whereby although cases share (albeit to varying extents) economic, social, and political features and geographical borders, we do not necessarily assume these cases are identical. Furthermore, as three researchers whom have lived and worked in England, we were also conscious of our own biases towards adopting an England-centric approach to our analysis. The overemphasis on England in the sport policy literature, is perhaps, in part, reflective of the broader political landscape within the UK, which appears to be 'Westminster' dominated and but also indicative of the sheer population imbalance that exists between the home nations (England: 56.2 million (84.3%), Scotland: 5.5 million (8.2%), Wales: 3.1 million (4.7%), Northern Ireland: 1.9 million (2.8%)). As a result, we have consciously set out to produce a volume of work that was equally reflective of sport policy and sport development across all home nations. On this point, we were also critically reflective

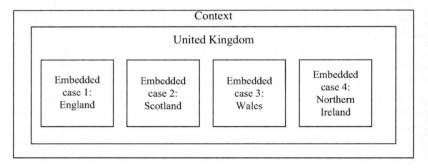

Figure 1.1 Embedded case study design to examine sport policy across the United Kingdom.

by giving the country chapter authors an opportunity to review and comment on our own work.

It is also for the above reasons that we deliberately sought out researchers who were experts in the sport policy field and were intimately familiar with the home nation in question. Whilst we recognise that working with an extended research team created additional methodological challenges, including issues regarding philosophical coherence (Mayan, 2009) and more practical coordination issues, we felt that this approach would ultimately enhance the validity of our study findings as each home nation contributor was directly involved with and connected to the larger project.

Finally, we wish to address the issue of generalisability. Explicitly, we recognise the obvious limitations of drawing any broader knowledge or theory from a comparative analysis of home nations across the UK. We fully appreciate that the policies, policy processes, programs, and challenges confronting sport development in each home nation are predominantly shaped by the social, cultural, and political structures of each nation. To further qualify the contribution of our study, we see two distinct ways in which this comparative analysis of home nations may have utility and be used more broadly in other contexts. First, the study exposes the rich history of sport across the UK and its historical cultural significance which, taken together, provide a useful comparator to evaluate the broad evolution of sport policy and the sport systems and structures of other Western democracies. Here, it would be useful to examine and compare each home nation's history and their systems and structures and to assess the extent to which these themes (e.g., complexity, fragmentation, the arrangements for and the effects of regional autonomy/devolution) are uniquely connected to certain contexts or largely consistent across a variety of contexts. Second, the study provides clear evidence of regional differences, cultural heterogeneity as well as the convergence and divergence of sport policy interests. In doing so, it provides evidence to support future studies that examine the national and/or regional distinctiveness of sport policy in countries with constituent components (e.g., Spain, Belgium, the Netherlands) as well as those that represent large federations (e.g., the USA, Canada, Germany). Such analyses can illuminate the inherent complexities and interdependencies that exist across sport policy in a nation state context. In this sense, we seek to build upon and extend previous comparative sport policy research (e.g., De Bosscher et al., 2015; Lindsey & Houlihan, 2013) so that both the similarities and differences of sport policies, processes, and practices across distinct geographical regions may be more closely examined and understood.

Analytical framework

We attempt to identify similarities and differences in sport policies, processes, and practices between home nations by applying a consistent analytical framework to each case. The framework itself was generated through drawing upon existing sport policy and development literature (see Appendix 2) with particular attention paid to the background/historical context, the evolution of sport policy, and the consideration of the specific policy domains relating to sport (e.g., elite, participation, and physical education/school sport). Each chapter begins within an overview of how sport and physical activity is organised and structured. Here, the authors were asked to identify what they considered to be unique to their home nation context. We also asked the authors to provide an overview of the key stakeholders and to discuss their interdependencies both within and beyond their home nation context. Next, in recognising the path-dependent nature of the policymaking process (North, 1990), we asked the authors to provide a brief overview of the evolution of sport policy and politics within their home nation. This section includes a discussion of the individual history and political context in which each home nation operates. Here we acknowledged that each home nation has its own sport policy and strategies and was at different stages in the policy development process. For example, at the time of writing, England had just released two ten-year strategies (Sport England's *Uniting a Movement Strategy* and UK Sport's *Strategic Plan 2021–2031*) and was in the formative stages of renewing its latest governmental policy (*Sporting Future*; DCMS, 2015). Similarly, in Northern Ireland, the Department for Communities was in the process of developing a new ten-year Sport and Physical Activity for Northern Ireland (*Active Living*; DfC, 2022), but its development had been inhibited by the COVID-19 pandemic. Following this, our framework focuses on specific policies relating to elite sport, mass participation (or community sport), and PE/school sport. The inclusion of the latter was particularly pertinent given the important role of PE/school sport in the development of the sport and physical activity policy agenda. These three sections follow a similar structure in that they provide an overview of key stakeholders and how the specific policy domain is organised. The final two sections focus on the specific policies and programmes that have been developed and a summary of the primary challenges and barriers for sport development within each home nation. Table 1.2 provides a summary of the key sections the make up the analytical framework.

Table 1.2 Analytical Framework

Section	Description
Overview and structure of sport	An overview of how sport and physical activity is organised and structured, identifying any unique features or characteristics within each home nation. This section will include an overview of the size and scope of country (demographics) and discuss the relationships and dependencies both within and across each home nation.
Brief evolution of sport policy and politics	A brief evolution of sport policy and politics within each home nation. This includes a discussion of the historical and political context in which each home nation operates and identifies some of the key trends and policy developments within each home nation.
Elite sport	An overview of how elite sport is structured, organised, and governed within the home nation. This includes the key organisations, agencies, and actors involved in overseeing and delivering sport and how each country identifies and develops talent, typical performance pathways and their role in developing elite athletes.
Participation and community sport	An overview of how community sport and physical activity is structured, organised, and governed within the home nation. This includes the key organisations, agencies, and actors involved in overseeing and delivering sport and physical activity objectives within each home nation.
Physical education and school sport	An overview of how physical education and school sport is structured, organised, and governed within the home nation. This includes the key organisations, agencies, and actors involved and their roles and responsibilities with supporting PE/school sport.
Sport development programmes and policies	A discussion of contemporary sport development and physical activity programmes and policies within each home nation including domestic campaigns, initiatives, and schemes that have been targeted at either increasing participation or identifying or developing talent.
Challenges and barriers to sport development	A discussion of the key challenges and barriers to developing sport and physical activity opportunities within the home nation including how the interconnections between home nations either enables or constraints the countries' ability to increase participation or produce medal success.
Summary	A brief summary of key findings and implications for future research.

Chapter summary

In summary, this chapter has outlined the broad parameters of the book including our rationale for undertaking a comparative study of this nature, size and scale. We have briefly described the broader historical and political context in which the four constituent home countries that make up the United Kingdom operate, recognising that many of these themes will be examined in more detail in the following chapters. Furthermore, in acknowledging that readers may not necessarily be familiar with the UK context, we have also outlined the unique characteristics (or peculiarities) of the United Kingdom, including discussing some of the broader themes such as nationalism, independence, and devolution. The latter part of this chapter provided an outline of the comparative methodological approach that we have adopted to guide an intra-country comparative analysis across the home nations. To this end, we have developed and articulated an analytical framework which was applied by our colleagues to each of their home nations. This not only provided a useful structuring device for analysing each of the four home nations individually but also enabled us to compare each case unit (i.e., home nation) to identify similarities and differences across these cases. What follows is an in-depth analysis of each of the home nations by contributors, beginning with England (Chapter 2) as this provides some useful broader political context for understanding the interrelations and dependencies that exist between England and other home nations. This is followed by Scotland (Chapter 3), Wales (Chapter 4), and Northern Ireland (Chapter 5). Our final chapter (Chapter 6) broadens the discussion to consider the themes that can be drawn from the country-specific analysis of each home nation as well as providing further consideration to the study limitations and identifying areas for future research.

At this point, we would also like to take this opportunity as editors of this volume to personally thank the contributors for their time and effort in producing valuable contributions to this ambitious project. Without their contributions, a comparative study of this nature simply would not have been possible.

Notes

1. Antrim, Armagh, Down, Fermanagh, Londonderry, and Tyrone.
2. As of 2022, Scotland have a devolved government and directly elected Parliament; Wales have a devolved government; Northern Ireland have a power sharing executive and directly elected assembly. As of 2020 there is an elected Welsh Parliament – so same as England – this needs to be changed further on as well.

3 The UK complete as Team GB (shorthand for Great Britain and Northern Ireland) in the summer, winter and youth Olympics and Paralympics and the majority of sport-specific continental and world championships. There are however historical arrangements that have resulted in home nation teams for example in football, rugby union, rugby league, cricket, and netball). The teams for the Commonwealth Games are predicated on the home nation.
4 For some sports, NGBs exist at both the home country and UK level (e.g., athletics, swimming), for others they only exist at the home country level (e.g., football, badminton) or at the UK level (e.g., wrestling).

References

Ancker, C. (2008). On the applicability of the most similar systems design and the most different systems design in comparative research. *International Journal of Social Research Methodology*, 11(5), 389–401.

Bairner, A. (2004). Inclusive soccer--Exclusive politics? Sports policy in Northern Ireland and the Good Friday Agreement. *Sociology of Sport Journal*, 21(3), 270–286.

Brailsford, D. (1991). *Sport, Time, and Society: The British at Play*. Routledge.

Byers, T., Slack, T., & Parent, M. (2012). *Key Concepts in Sport Management*. Sage.

Cairney, P. (2019). *Understanding Public Policy: Theories and Issues*. Red Globe Press.

DCMS. (2015). *Sporting Future: A New Strategy for an Active Nation*. DCMS.

De Bosscher, V., Shibli, S., Westerbeek, H., & Van Bottenberg, M. (2015). *Successful Elite Sport Policies: An International Comparison of the Sports Policy Factors Leading to International Sporting Success (SPLISS 2.0) in 15 Nations*. Meyer and Meyer.

De Leon, P. (1999). The stages approach to the policy process: What has it done? Where is it going? In P. Sabatier (Eds.), *Theories of the Policy Process* (pp. 19–34). Westview Press.

Della Porta, D. (2008). Comparative analysis: Case-oriented versus variable-oriented research. In D. Della Porta & M. Keating (Eds.), *Approaches and Methodologies in the Social Sciences: A Pluralist Perspective* (pp. 198–222). Cambridge University Press.

Department for Communities. (2022). *Sport and Physical Activity Strategy NI*. Department for Communities.

Dogan, M., & Pélassy, D. (1990). *How to Compare Nations: Strategies in Comparative Politics*. Chatham House.

Dougall, A. (2011). *The Devil's Book: Charles I, the Book of Sports and Puritanism in Tudor and Early Stuart England*. University of Exeter Press.

Dowling, M., Brown, P., Legg, D., & Grix, J. (2018). Deconstructing comparative sport policy analysis: Assumptions, challenges, and new directions. *International Journal of Sport Policy and Politics*, 10(4), 687–704.

Dowling, M., & Harris, S. (2021). *Comparing Sporting Nations: Theory and Method*. Meyer & Meyer Sport.

Galloway, B. (1986). *The Union of England and Scotland, 1603–1608*. J. Donald.
Gilroy, P. (2004). *After Empire: Melancholia Or Convivial Culture?* Routledge.
Harris, S., Mori, K., & Collins, M. (2009). Great expectations: Voluntary sports clubs and their role in delivering national policy for English sport. *VOLUNTAS: International Journal of Voluntary and Nonprofit Organizations*, 20(4), 405–423.
Hassan, D., & Telford, R. (2014). Sport and community integration in Northern Ireland. *Sport in Society*, 17(1), 89–101.
Hitchen, P. (2008). *The Abolition of Britain*. Quartet.
HM Government. (2014). Scottish independence referendum. Retrieved from: https://www.gov.uk/government/topical-events/scottish-independence-referendum/about.
HM Government. (2019). Devolution of powers to Scotland, Wales and Northern Ireland. Retrieved from: https://www.gov.uk/guidance/devolution-of-powers-to-scotland-wales-and-northern-ireland.
Hoekman, R., & Scheerder, J. (2021). Sport policy practice and outcome; theoretical and empirical approaches. *European Journal for Sport and Society*, 18(2), 103–113.
Holt, R. (Ed.). (1990). *Sport and the Working Class in Modern Britain*. Manchester University Press.
Houlihan, B. (1997). *Sport, Policy, and Politics: A Comparative Analysis*. Routledge.
Houlihan, B. (2005). Public sector sport policy: Developing a framework for analysis. *International Review for the Sociology of Sport*, 40(2), 163–185.
https://www.communities-ni.gov.uk/sites/default/files/publications/communities/dfc-active-living-sport-physical-strategy-northern-ireland.pdf [Accessed 29/06/22].
Jarvie, G., & Reid, I. A. (1999). Scottish sport, nationalist politics and culture. *Sport in Society*, 2(2), 22–43.
Jowell, R. (1998). How comparative is comparative research? *American Behavioral Scientist*, 42(2), 168–177.
Keating, M. (2019). Scotland and the Battle of the Unions: Independence over Kingdom? Nationalworld. Retrieved from: https://theglobepost.com/2019/05/02/scotland-independence-brexit/.
Kumar, K. (2000). Nation and Empire: English and British National Identity in a comparative perspective. *Theory and Society*, 29(5), 575–608.
Kumar, K. (2010). Negotiating English identity: Englishness, Britishness, and the future of the United Kingdom. *Nations and Nationalism*, 16(3), 469–487.
Landman, T., & Carvalho, E. (2017). *Issues and Methods in Comparative Politics* (4th ed.). Routledge.
Lijphart, A. (1971). Comparative politics and the comparative method. *American Political Science Review*, 65(3), 682–693.
Lindsey, I., & Houlihan, B. (2013). *Sport Policy in Britain*. Routledge.
Macfarlane, J. (2021, 25 May). What are the arguments for Scottish independence? Experts explain the reasons why Scotland would vote 'Yes'. Nationalworld. Retrieved from: https://www.nationalworld.com/news/politics/what-are-

the-arguments-for-scottish-independence-experts-explain-the-reasons-why-scotland-would-vote-yes-3249855.
Mackintosh, C. (2011). An analysis of County Sports Partnerships in England: The fragility, challenges and complexity of partnership working in sports development. *International Journal of Sport Policy and Politics*, 3(1), 45–64.
Mackintosh, C., & Liddle, J. (2015). Emerging school sport development policy, practice and governance in England: Big Society, autonomy and decentralisation. *Education 3–13*, 43(6), 603–620.
Mayan, M. (2009). *Essentials of Qualitative Inquiry*. Routledge. https://doi.org/10.4324/9781315429250.
Nairn, T. (2000). *After Britain: New Labour and the Return of Scotland*. Granta.
McInch, A., & Fleming, S. (2022). Sport policy formation and enactment in post-devolution Wales: 1999–2020. *International Journal of Sport Policy and Politics*, 14(2), 225–237.
North, D. C. (1990). *Institutions, Institutional Change and Economic Performance*. Cambridge University Press.
Øyen, E. (1990). *Comparative Methodology: Theory and Practice in International Social Research*. Sage.
Przeworski, A., & Teune, H. (1970). *The Logic of Comparative Social Inquiry*. Wiley-Interscience.
Ragin, C. (2014). *The Comparative Method: Moving beyond Qualitative and Quantitative Strategies*. University of California Press.
Reid, F. (2012). Increasing sports participation in Scotland: Are voluntary sports clubs the answer? *International Journal of Sport Policy and Politics*, 4(2), 221–241.
Reid, G. (2009). Delivering sustainable practice? A case study of the Scottish Active Schools programme. *Sport, Education and Society*, 14(3), 353–370.
Sartori, G. (1970). Concept misinformation in comparative politics. *American Political Science Review*, 64(4), 1033–1053. https://doi.org/10.2307/1958356.
Schuster, J. M. (2007). Participation studies and cross-national comparison: Proliferation, prudence, and possibility. *Cultural Trends*, 16(2), 99–196.
Scottish National Party. (2016). *Re-elect: The Scottish National Party Manifesto*. Scottish National Party.
Sim, P. (2021, 9 May). Scottish independence: Could the Supreme Court rule on a referendum? BBC. Retrieved from: https://www.bbc.com/news/uk-scotland-scotland-politics-57047898.
Stafford, J. (2022). *The Enlightenment Critique of Empire in Ireland c. 1750–1776*. Cambridge University Press.
The Scottish Parliament. (2017). Scotland's Choice. Retrieved from: S5M-04710 | Scottish Parliament Website [Accessed 01/06/22].
Thompson, A., Bloyce, D., & Mackintosh, C. (2021). "It is always going to change" – Examining the experiences of managing top-down changes by sport development officers working in national governing bodies of sport in England. *Managing Sport and Leisure*, 26(1–2), 60–79.
Yin, R. (2017). *Case Study Research: Design and Methods* (7th ed.). Sage.

2 Sport Policy in England

Iain Lindsey and Daniel Bloyce

Overview and structure of sport

England is the largest of the home nations within the United Kingdom (UK), in terms of both geography (130,279 km^2) and population (56.5 m). Despite the political complexity within the UK, since 1998, sport policy has been considered a devolved matter for the respective home nations. However, as was made clear by the Department for Digital, Culture, Media and Sport (DCMS) and Strategy Unit in the publication of *Game Plan* in 2002, "it is not possible to undertake a review of English sports policy, structures and systems without considering the wider UK position" (p. 21).

The DCMS (Department for Digital, Culture, Media and Sport) is the government department that has responsibility for sport in the UK. However, although sport is a devolved matter, interestingly the DCMS still has a specific remit for sport in England, even though it is a 'British' government department. The DCMS then funds sport in England, most notably through both the UK and English Sports Councils. As non-departmental public bodies, the Sports Councils have held a central position in the structure for sport in the UK since their inception in the early 1970s. However, over the first decade or so, concern was frequently expressed that the bigger decisions favoured England and English sport. As such, and in connection with an increasing focus on 'modernising' the systems and structures of sport in the UK, a significant reorganisation of sport occurred (Houlihan & Green, 2009). Initially this was under John Major's government, but then especially under Tony Blair's Labour government in 1997. This saw the establishment of Sport England and UK Sport. The responsibility for Sport England was primarily with grassroots sport, and general participation, which left elite sport under the broad focus of UK Sport – and this has remained the areas of focus ever since.

DOI: 10.4324/9781003241232-2

Even still, some aspects of elite sport remain home-nation focused, and the establishment of the English Institute of Sport (EIS) in 2002 really underlines this. The EIS plays a significant part in supporting and funding elite-level, English athletes in many (mostly Olympic and Paralympic) sports.

More locally, Sport England funds a network of Active Partnerships (formerly known as County Sport Partnerships) to promote physical activity in communities throughout the country. Active Partnerships typically work with a range of organisations, including local authorities. Local authorities have focused much less on servicing sport, with many local authority development units closing down, especially with similar work being undertaken in the Active Partnerships over the last 20 years, and growing cuts to local authority budgets generally. Nevertheless, local authorities still provide the vast majority of places and spaces where physical activity and sport participation take place, continuing to be one of the largest providers of facility space in England.

Finally, the National Governing Bodies of Sport (NGBs) continue to play a key role – not only in providing systems for elite performers but also in enabling the continued development of grassroots sport.

Brief evolution of sport policy and politics

Examining sport policy and politics in England in isolation from the other home nations is especially difficult. At different points in time, there have been different government policies that have impacted sport across the UK or specific home nations while not affecting others. We start with a brief overview of sport policy from the 1960s, following the publication of the *Wolfenden Report*.

In 1960, the Central Council of Physical Recreation (CCPR) published the *Wolfenden Report*, helped to raise the profile of sport within government and also provided "the context within which public involvement in sport was to be considered for the next generation" (Houlihan & White, 2002, p. 18). The *Report* highlighted a major concern at the dramatic drop-off in participation in sport and physical activity at school-leaving age. In addition, the *Report* recommended the establishment of a Sports Council to oversee sport in the UK. Whilst not acted upon by the then Conservative government, the Scottish Sports Council and the Sports Council for Wales were established with Royal Charter statutes in December 1971 and February 1972, respectively. A Great Britain Sports Council, which would also have specific responsibility for England, was also established in the summer of 1972.

In 1975, the British government published the first White Paper on sport entitled *Sport and Recreation*. Among many other things, the government distinguished between "sport" and "recreation", with the former being regarded as the performance and excellence dimension of sports development work, and the latter said to be more concerned with mass participation (Bloyce & Smith, 2010). The reorientation of policy towards focusing upon identified target groups contributed to the Sports Council's focus on 'Sport for All'. Such an approach was especially prominent in England in the late 1970s and early 1980s, and numerous programmes in England were increasingly focused on using sport to address a variety of wider social issues. The Sports Council argued that "not to tackle the needs of these groups would put the Council in breach of its Royal Charter" (Sports Council, 1982, p. 7), and this has been a consistent theme in English sport policy since (Bloyce & Smith, 2010).

Upon victory at the 1992 General Election, John Major's government established the Department of National Heritage (DNH), which included sport. In 1994, a National Lottery was introduced and this has since provided substantial additional funds to sport that were not previously available and helped change the landscape of sport policy in England, and the UK more widely. Strict targets related to the release of funding on a regular cycle have been a pattern of sport policy in England ever since (Thompson et al., 2021).

In July 1994, there was a separation of the Sports Council into a UK Sports Council and an English Sports Council, while the other home nation Councils remained unchanged. This development was swiftly followed by the publication of a second government White Paper on sport, *Sport: Raising the Game* (DNH, 1995). Amongst other things, the paper outlined the need for a more efficient structure for the organisation of sport in England. UK Sport and Sport England were eventually established by Royal Charter in January 1997. One of the key reasons for this restructuring was to "eradicate the anomaly of the former Sports Council having both British and English functions", but the overall, unintended, "outcome was the bifurcation of sports development" (Houlihan & White, 2002, p. 70). UK Sport was to oversee provision for elite sport, whereas Sport England was to focus more on increasing participation – though still with a view, in the old traditional sports development continuum model, of producing the next generation of elite-level athletes.

One key policy development in England was the establishment of County Sports Partnerships (CSPs). Forty-five such partnerships were rolled out starting in 1999. A significant feature of Labour government policy was 'joined-up thinking' (Bloyce & Smith, 2010), and this was reflected in Sport England's funding of CSPs as a network of local partnerships designed to increase sport and physical activity participation. Soon after CSPs were established, in December 2002, the DCMS and the government's Strategy Unit published *Game Plan*, which, it was acknowledged, "concentrates on government sports policy and delivery in England" (DCMS/Strategy Unit, 2002, p. 21). Central within *Game Plan* was a focus on health and community outcomes at a local level, whilst retaining a focus on elite sport for national governing bodies of sport as well as school and youth sport.

Game Plan also established a practice that started in 2005 for all NGBs in receipt of Sport England funding to produce 'Whole Sport Plans' (WSPs) every four years to provide details and specific targets to be achieved to qualify for Sport England funding in the next cycle (Thompson et al., 2021). A key aspect of these targets was, for some NGBs, medal success at international competitions but also sport participation rates. To measure changes in sport participation, Sport England created the *Active People Survey* (APS) in 2005. The survey was an attempt to provide "robust baseline data on participation rates, better understanding of barriers to participation and more information on local demographics linked to participation" (Sport England, 2004, p. 19). There has been much debate about the value of such data (HM Government, 2015), but it has contributed significantly to the landscape of sport policy in England ever since, with various organisations using the data with a view to justify policy and seek funding. As an indication of the direction of travel, at least for grassroots sport policy in England, the APS was re-branded the Active Lives Survey in 2016. This was to reflect the greater importance that the government was placing on the wider role of activity in people's lives, not just sports participation. Another reflection of this broader focus was when the CSP network was re-branded as the Active Partnerships Network in 2019.

After the hosting of the London Olympics in 2012, the subsequent and most recent government policy impacting on sport in England, *Sporting Future*, published in December 2015, further captures this growing focus on physical activity as being a key aim of government sport policy. Target groups that had been a 'wicked problem' for successive governments, in terms of low participation rates, were, once again, the stated focus of the strategy: "We will distribute funding to focus on those people who tend not to take part in sport, including women and girls, disabled people, those in lower socio-economic groups and older people" (HM Government, 2015, p. 10). However, the strategy clarified that "funding decisions will be made on the basis of the social good that sport and physical activity can deliver, not simply on the number of participants" (HM Government, 2015, p. 10). *Sport for All?* was published by Sport England in January 2020 with a specific focus on, once again, promoting sports participation among Black, Asian, and Minority Ethnic (BAME) groups, which was, amongst others, proving to be a 'wicked problem' for those engaged in equality and diversity issues in sport policy in England. A renewed focus on sport for social good was further emphasised in order to address the impact of COVID-19. Sport England produced a ten-year strategy in 2021, *Uniting the Movement*. In this strategy, the then CEO of Sport England, Tim Hollingsworth stated, "we *now* understand that what's happening in our lives day to day, and in the places we live and work, are much bigger factors" on physical activity and sports participation (emphasis added, Sport England, 2021, p. 4). Of course, academics have long been pointing out the need to understand the wider socioeconomic influences on sport and physical activity participation rates (Bloyce & Smith, 2010). The impact that the wider focus on the social good of sport, and how that might be measured, and also the fact that this policy continues, unsurprisingly, to focus on perhaps more non-traditional physical activity outlets prompted in *Sporting Future* will be interesting to examine over the ensuing years.

Elite sport

The emergence of state-sponsored, elite sport development 'systems' is an increasingly prominent feature of sport policy in numerous countries throughout the world. The British government had been labelled a "late adopter" of elite sport development systems (Green & Houlihan, 2005, p. 63), primarily as following the start of global sport competitions in the late 19th and early 20th centuries, the British government took an 'amateur gentleman' attitude to sports performance. It was not considered an area in which government should meddle. Developments, particularly in the 1990s, contributed to something of a sea change in the attitude of successive governments. The introduction of the National Lottery in 1994 provided funding, hitherto unavailable in such significant sums, to support elite athletes in sports outside of some of the more traditional, commercially successful team sports. In addition, the widely regarded poor medal return at the Atlanta Olympic Games in 1996 proved to be a 'focusing event' (Chalip, 1995) for the British government, and policy attention was devoted to elite sport – and related processes of talent identification. Arguably, these policies have proven highly successful, at least within the summer Olympic and Paralympic Games, as Team GB have finished in the top four in the medals tables at the last four Olympic and Paralympic Games starting with a fourth placed finish at the 2008 Olympics and second placed finish at the Paralympics in Beijing.

Undoubtedly, trends in the wider UK elite sport policy picture over the last 20 years or so have been significantly influenced by developments within England specifically. After a number of years of political wrangling, the English Institute of Sport (EIS) was eventually opened in May 2002. Today, the EIS is owned and funded by UK Sport and is made up of eight world centres for the support of elite-level athletes. Clearly, a key aspect of the services provided is to offer sport science support to current athletes, but also those with potential to succeed on the world stage. UK Sport have their general policy approach to this in the shape of their performance pathway models: World class Podium, World class Podium Potential, and Performance Foundations, which focus on athletes at different stages of their elite-level career. To this end, numerous talent identification programmes have been put in place over the last 20 years as the UK Sport and the EIS attempted to look for the next generation of English elite performers.

Talent identification policies and programmes in England have tended to focus on identifying talent through the club systems with coaches identifying existing athletes to put forward into such programmes – often working alongside the relevant NGB. There have been national searches for talent focusing on anthropometrical and performance measures to identify talent. For example, the *Sporting Giants* programme in 2007 sought to attract tall people to try out to become potential rowers for future Games. Other programmes have focused on talent transfer. *Pitch 2 Podium*, for example, attempted to encourage athletes that were not progressing within the professional football academy system to try out within different Olympic sports. More recently, *From Home 2 The Games* commenced in 2021 focusing on attracting young people from across "all communities" (UK Sport, n.d.) to try activities that they may never have thought about getting involved with before. Emphasis was also placed on enjoying sport. Perhaps this was a response to the growing negative perception in some circles, notably the English press, towards the previously acknowledged ruthless approach to funding, which had led to some claims of a win at all costs and bullying atmosphere in some sports.

The 'no compromise' approach that had been adopted in UK sport elite policy since the advent of the EIS (Bloyce & Smith, 2010; Green, 2007) epitomised this ruthless approach to achieving medal success at international competitions. Funding was narrowly focused only on those sports and athletes that were deemed to have a realistic chance of medal success. This policy was pursued to such a degree that there is some evidence that policy funding was diverted away from grassroots policy, increasingly towards pursuit of medal success (Lovett & Bloyce, 2017). This also had significant impacts on some NGBs, whose funding was cut following perceived lack of success, especially when most of these NGBs were largely ill-prepared to react to such cuts (Bostock et al., 2018). The apparent justification for funding elite sport was captured in *Sporting Future*, where it was stated, without any supporting evidence, that such medal success "provides significant wellbeing, social and economic benefits to the nation. Put simply, the more our teams win, the better the nation feels" (HM Government, 2015, p. 43). Within the policy, HM Government (2015, p. 43) also stated that there was "no reason to change" the current approach to elite sport in England and that they would ensure policies would "continue to be focused on the needs of the system". Despite the stated support for this approach, in the years since *Sporting Future* was published, and in response to considerable negative media coverage and 'whistle blowing' from within some sports (notably, cycling, gymnastics, and swimming) about a culture of bullying and abuse, some sports have sought to re-evaluate the focus they have placed on their 'no compromise' approach to success. A clear example of this is in the publication of the *Whyte Review* (2022) on British Gymnastics, which led to British Gymnastics, for example, publishing *Reform '25* where it was explicitly stated that they had seemingly lost sight of the need to focus on athlete welfare and well-being in the pursuit of medal success. It will be interesting to see how such 'new' approaches play out, especially when the funding model for Olympic success still seems like it will be primarily based on medal success at future Games.

Participation and community sport

Policies for adult participation and community sport in England have followed a very different trajectory than those for elite sport, as well as those for PE and school sport which are covered in the next section. The prioritisation of 'sport for all' policies in the 1970s, during which significant facility building contributed to increasing participation, represents a period of policy effectiveness that stands in marked contrast to the inconsistent policy direction and stagnant participation rates that have mostly marked subsequent decades. The goals of policies directed towards community sport have been varied, but can also be recognised to have changed at times from, for example, seeking to achieve a variety of wider social policy goals through the early 2000s, through a period of 'sport for sport's sake' signified by the *Playing to Win* (DCMS, 2008) strategy from 2008 to 2012, to a subsequent shift since 2015 again towards a range of social outcomes amongst which health has been particularly prominent. Policies have concomitantly veered between focusing on sport specifically and then becoming inclusive of the wider promotion of physical activity. As a result, particular policy initiatives, and the targets associated with them, have often been relatively short term, with the changes that have come at intervals of three to five years being reflective of, and contributing to, a lack of long-term success in addressing entrenched low and unequal participation across England (Houlihan & Lindsey, 2012).

The role of national stakeholders may be considered as particularly significant in the failures of participation and community sport policy. Houlihan and Lindsey (2012) argue that successive governments have been the primary culprits for inconsistent and ineffective policies, with periods of governmental neglect of participation and community sport interspersed with ministerial interventions which have sought to re-orientate policy in a new direction. The inconsistencies in governmental policies and approaches have most immediately affected Sport England. Throughout numerous reorganisations of their funding programmes and organisational structures, two elements of Sport England's approach remained relatively consistent from the turn of this century through to an emergent turn in strategic direction from 2016 onwards. First, Sport England have maintained a primarily topdown approach based on tight specifications for the programmes and organisations that they have funded, which has been accompanied by national prescription of targets by which the performance of those in receipt of funding has been measured. Second, the position of NGBs as the key set of organisations that Sport England works with and funds has largely been maintained over time. Despite common weaknesses in NGBs' planning and capability to develop community sport participation (Harris & Houlihan, 2016), their historically privileged national position was still exemplified by their collective receipt of over a third of all funding awarded by Sport England from 2012 to 2016 (Sport England, 2016).

By contrast, the two types of local organisation with roles in the provision and development of sport across the whole of England – namely, local authorities and Active Partnerships – have suffered from being accorded relatively weaker positions in the implementation of community sport and participation policies. Local authorities' capacity to offer provision and support to develop community sport has declined through general constraints placed on them by national governments as much as the relative neglect of local authorities by sport policy and decision makers particularly. This has perhaps been most clearly illustrated through the decade from 2010 to 2020 during which extreme austerity imposed by central governments on local authorities led to average cuts of 70% in their spending on sport and recreation (Institute of Fiscal Studies, 2019), with resultant closures of local facilities and the widespread disappearance of sports development as a function within local authorities. Challenges faced by the network of Active Partnerships that span England have been somewhat different, with their core funding provided by Sport England. Thus, Active Partnerships have found their roles consistently shifting according to the different orientation of national sport policies over time. Their early positioning as a local fulcrum supporting NGBs' efforts to increase participation and the consistent necessity to work to objectives set by Sport England has largely limited the possibilities for Active Partnerships to develop distinctive strategies that could address local needs and contexts in the particular areas in which they work (Grix & Phillpots, 2011; Harris & Houlihan, 2016).

Recently, however, national sport policies in England have begun another shift towards a more localised and place-based approaches to strategic development of community sport and physical activity, which has, to an extent, rebalanced the relative prioritisation of NGBs, local authorities, and Active Partnerships highlighted above. The beginnings of this shift may be traced to the government's 2015 *Sporting Future* strategy and Sport England's 2016 *Towards an Active Nation* strategy, but it was the allocation of around £100m of Sport England funding to 12 Local Delivery Pilots from 2017 onwards, which was a first concrete marker of a more localised approach to community sport. The influence of these pilots was evident not only in their renewed funding in 2021 but also in the publication of Sport England's *Uniting the Movement* strategy of the same year in which they committed to "a more bottom-up approach to our work and investment. Working with – not doing things to – communities, and helping those affected to play a role in what happens in their neighbourhood and how it gets done" (Sport England, 2021, p. 22).

At the time of writing, however, it remains to be seen to what extent this shift towards greater localism substantively replaces previous top-down approaches and provides the consistency required to alleviate the institutional problems identified in this section. Recovery from the COVID-19 pandemic has also been a priority in the sport sector, which also has significant implications in terms of support for local provision. However, previous political encouragement for more locally influenced policy development has largely proved to be false dawns. Moreover, the wider history examined in this section indicates the need for caution in any assessment of whether community and participation sport policies may have the longevity that would be a prerequisite to make headway in shifting long-term trends of inactivity.

Physical education and school sport

Distinctive periods of English PE and school sport (PESS) policies can be identified through the time of the Labour governments, first elected in 1997, and then Conservative-led governments from 2010 onwards. It was the former Labour governments that began significant investment in PESS in the early 2000s (Houlihan & Green, 2006). Historically high levels of funding have continued under Conservative-led governments from 2013, and it is the period of relative continuity in PESS policy since then that will be the main focus of this section. While the approach to PESS policy implementation pursued by Conservative-led governments from 2013 differed significantly from that of earlier Labour governments, initially it is relevant to note the extent of consistency across these two periods in respect to broader policy goals for PESS. Common aspirations expressed through ongoing government rhetoric, documentation, and association with particular funding initiatives have sought to orientate PESS towards a variety of wider social policy agendas, such as education attainment and, to an increasing extent, health (Lindsey, 2020). Meanwhile, in an underlying but potentially contradictory trend, successive governments have also generally accorded a higher degree of prioritisation to school-based competitive sport than the educational ethos which many PE professionals and academics would have preferred (Lindsey et al., 2021).

This relative weighting of policy goals for PESS is identifiable in repeated revisions of the National Curriculum for Physical Education (NCPE), the most recent of which occurred in 2013. The influence of rising concerns with the health of young people is evident in the emphasis of the 2013 NCPE towards increasing levels of activity and fitness through PE lessons, as well as the importance placed on children developing fundamental movement skills (which some consider to be a component of physical literacy). Inherent tensions remained, however, with the ongoing prominence that the revised NCPE gave to competition which was rhetorically justified as part of the 2012 London Olympics legacy (DfE, 2013). That the 2013 curriculum was also less prescriptive for schools than previous iterations also fit with the Conservatives' overall education policies, through which an increasing proportion of state-funded schools were exempted from requirements to teach the National Curriculum specifically.

The policy approach evident through and associated with the NCPE has had implications for the subject, especially in secondary schools. Harris (2018, p. 2) indicates that governmental prioritisation of English, maths, and science subjects has brought the consequence that other subjects "such as physical education tend[s] to be marginalised and 'squeezed' in terms of time and resource" in schools. Although this impact may have been somewhat mitigated and blurred by the policy impetus for primary school PESS, there has not been concomitant governmental priority accorded to PESS in secondary schools. Moreover, under Conservative government changes instigated in 2010, secondary schools have also lost their key positioning in the organisational system of School Sport Partnerships created by the preceding Labour government. Ultimately, the decline in the hours of PE taught nationally in a typical week in secondary schools from 333,800 in November 2010 to 281,572 in November 2018 (House of Commons Library, 2019) is reflective of what may be considered a degree of policy neglect.

In contrast, governmental policy for PESS in primary schools has been advanced since 2013 through considerable funding for the PE and Sport Premium. The initial announcement of national funding of £150m per annum for the PE and Sport Premium came after London's hosting of the 2012 Olympics had led to significant media attention towards concerns that the then Conservative-led government lacked commitment to school and youth sport after their earlier withdrawal of funding for Labour's School Sport Partnerships system (Lindsey, 2020). Since then, funding for the PE and Sport Premium has not only been repeatedly renewed, but from 2017/2018 overall funding was doubled to £320m annually through the allocation of additional income generated by the Soft Drinks Industry Levy which was implemented as a 'Sugar Tax' on the sale of drinks containing added sugar. Through this funding, all state-funded primary schools in England receive a baseline of £16,000 per annum with a smaller proportion of additional money based on their number of pupils. Decisions on spending PE and Sport Premium funds are, therefore, largely devolved to individual primary schools in what is a universal and straightforward approach to distributing funding, but one which Lindsey et al. (2021, p. 285) indicate takes "no account of potentially different degrees of need within primary schools or of existing inequalities in participation" in PE, sport, and physical activity.

Over time, further debates over the orientation and the short- and longer-term implications of the PE and Sport Premium have also continued. The decision to focus funding on primary schools was relatively uncontroversial at the outset with there being a widespread consensus within and beyond government regarding the limitations of provision and teacher capacity in primary schools (Lindsey, 2020). Consequently, it is perhaps unsurprising that various studies have identified that much of the overall spending from schools' PE and Sport Premium has gone towards employing additional and external staff (DfE, 2019; Griggs, 2016; Lindsey et al., 2021). As a result of this form of spending, widespread expansion of a multiplicity of companies and other non-profit organisations offering services and coaches to support and deliver PE and sport in primary schools has occurred. Critics of the PE and Sport Premium have, therefore, questioned the extent of long-term strategic coordination for local PE and school sport provision, the potential replacement of teaching professionals with sport coaches (Griggs & Randall, 2019; Jones & Green, 2017), and the lack of regulation of external providers and lack of accountability in the use of PE and Sport Premium spending (Lindsey et al., 2021). Nevertheless, at the time of writing, the prospects of a(ny) government with a multiplicity of other priorities finding the impetus and bandwidth to address these problems through a systematic redevelopment of PESS policy looks remote.

Sport development programmes and policies

Contemporary sports development policy and practice in England mixes similarities of the historical origins and trends in this field, with organisational features that are very different to the past. In terms of the former, the most commonly cited reference point for the historical emergence of sports development were the 15 'Action Sport' programmes that were instigated in areas of London and the West Midlands as a part of the government's response to riots that occurred in various urban communities across England in the summer of 1981 (Houlihan & White, 2002). Funding for the Action Sport programmes came jointly from the (then) British Sports Council and the Manpower Services Commission, a non-departmental public body responsible for employment and training services. Utilisation of external funding designated for social policy purposes is not the only connection with contemporary sports development, with their there also being recent relevance in Hargreaves' (1986, p. 225) recognition of Action Sport programmes representing a shift towards "resources [being] concentrated more on the problems of 'deprived areas' that is, on preventing vandalism and delinquency [and] dealing with the consequences of unemployment" also holding resonance.

As an alternative and subsequent point of departure, the late 1990s and 2000s represents a period in which significant resources provided by the Labour government, the organisation, and the scale and scope of sports development grew significantly. Sports development teams and roles were commonplace within local authorities' portfolio of services such that there could be considered an aspect of universalism to sports development even if practice may have been differentially focused on specific local and national priorities (Houlihan & White, 2002). The proliferation of sport-specific development roles supported by or within the structures of many NGBs also represented something of a 'mainstreaming' of sports development at the time (Green, 2009). The further instigation of specific national initiatives directed towards addressing wider social issues perhaps had greater resonance with the preceding Action Sport programmes. Amongst such initiatives, Positive Futures was the programme that potentially had greatest national prominence in bringing together national support and resources from the Home Office, Youth Justice Board, and Sport England to deliver localised projects in England and Wales that sought to use sport to foster social inclusion and provide alternative pathways for young people (Houlihan & White, 2002).

The advent of a period of national fiscal austerity by the Conservative-led coalition government that was in power from 2010 signified another recalibration in the focus and organisation of sports development (Widdop et al., 2019). Ongoing trends for local authorities to shift away from direct provision of sport and leisure services were combined with the budget cuts indicated earlier in the chapter, leading to widespread retrenchment away from sports development being a funded service and a specific occupational role within councils (Mori et al., in press). Instead, what became more emergent for sports development may be considered to be surprisingly akin to Prime Minister David Cameron's otherwise abandoned 'Big Society' ideal of community and civil society activism, with a reconfiguration of sports development occurring again with the emergence of a new and expanding range of sport-focused voluntary (or third) sector organisations.

Amongst these organisations, national charities such as StreetGames and Sported particularly grew in prominence and importance nationally, while working with and supporting networks of local organisations involved with community-based sport and physical activity provision. Funding for such organisations came from Sport England (2016, p. 10) who had, after years of focusing their support towards NGBs, remarkably admitted that they had "only a few proven delivery models and providers we can confidently back". As the impetus for and within this emergent sector of national charities and local community organisations grew, the terminology connecting it altered towards that of 'sport-for-development' which represented the wider social purposes to which many organisations and their programmes became directed.

Walker and Hayton's (2018) research across a variety of such sport-for-development organisations is particularly valuable in illuminating both the potential and problems of this latest variant of sports development. The diversity that exists across sport-for-development organisations can be seen as both a strength and a weakness. On the one hand, the range of different social objectives that sport-for-development organisations collectively address is combined with commonly flexible and innovative approaches that lead them to be well placed to address social policy objectives in local communities. On the other hand, the sustainability of such organisations and their provision can be dependent on continually accessing new sources of funding, which can be draining on organisational capacity; can leave them overly dependent on the unpredictability of politics and funding streams; and potentially lead to 'mission drift' (Walker & Hayton, 2018). The associated requirement to continually demonstrate impact, often in quantitative terms, is also representative of the ongoing encroachment of business-oriented practices within sports development. Returning to the opening of this section, the focus of many sport-for-development organisations on areas of deprivation reflects both their orientation towards greatest need and a retreat from more universal models of sports development towards one characterised more by fragmentation (Mori et al., *in press*).

Challenges and barriers to sport development

An important point of departure for any consideration of the challenges facing sports development is an appraisal of the successes and failures of past approaches. The clearest area of success is in elite sport, in which there has been a continuation of those policies (described earlier) which have repeatedly been effective in delivering strong medal-winning performances by Team GB through Olympic and Paralympic cycles through to Tokyo 2020(+1). In other areas of sport policy and development in England, the picture is far less positive. Overall rates of sport participation showed a fall by around 4.5% from 1991 to 2015 (Weed, 2016). While the gap between male and female participation has decreased somewhat, socio-economic and other inequalities across sport and physical activity remain substantial, deep-rooted, and exacerbated by the pandemic (Sport England, 2022). It is harder to assess the impact of PE and sport policies due to the lack of comprehensive national data. However, despite almost nine years of significant PE and Sport Premium funding, there are major concerns about the delivery and quality of primary school provision (House of Lords, 2021), and the government's own data shows a concerning decrease in the time allocated to PE in secondary schools (see Lindsey et al., 2021).

These issues present different challenges for those responsible and working in sport policy and development at different levels. The governmental structure in which the DCMS oversees the delivery of elite and community sport policy objectives by UK Sport and Sport England, respectively, masks differential complexity across these different areas. As De Bosscher and van Bottenburg (2011, p. 582) remarked some time ago, "elite sport has developed into a relatively autonomous world", and, in that regard, UK Sport has benefited from and engineered a self-contained organisational system to deliver Olympic and Paralympic medals. Moreover, Houlihan and Lindsey (2012) argue that the presence of a tight-knit coalition of stakeholders advocating for prioritisation of elite sport has supported the ongoing scale of funding prioritised towards Olympic and Paralympic success, which has been maintained even over recent periods in which wider austerity has affected many other aspects of public funding, including community sport and recreation.

On the other hand, Coalter's (2013, p. 7) argument that "the determinants of sports participation lie well beyond the realms of sport policy" in part reflects the greater extent to which grassroots sports for both adults and young people are situated at a nexus of cross-governmental responsibilities. Potential contributions to the most recent government policy, *Sporting Future*, were recognised across nine different governmental departments (HM Government, 2015), and the commitment in this policy document to a "genuinely cross-government approach" (p. 12) represents an aspiration that is as long-standing as it is challenging. A recent report by a House of Lords (2021) committee highlights the challenge of responsibility for sport policy being situated in a relatively small government department (DCMS), while other departments, such as those responsible for health and education, may hold and offer far greater resources but do not have sport and physical activity as institutionalised priorities within their wider scope of policy responsibilities. The explicit orientation of *Sporting Future* (HM Government, 2015) to achieve a set of five wider social and economic outcomes through sport reflects this degree of policy overlap, but also can obscure where responsibilities for delivering on sport policy aspirations lie.

The fragmentation of responsibilities for sports development and policy implementation at other levels is equally a long-standing and intractable challenge. Whilst remaining a key provider or facilitator of opportunities for sport participation and physical activity, the impetus from English local authorities has been constrained by the extent to which austerity has limited budgets and also the status of sport as a non-statutory service which is often marginalised in comparison with other local policy priorities. Coordination across other key organisations, especially Active Partnerships and NGBs, is also subject to institutionalised challenges. Active Partnerships vary considerably in (population) size, and so their resources, extent of national and local influence, and the possibilities of local coordination also inevitably vary as a result. Similarly, the scale of national resources allocated to different NGBs varies considerably, as does their institutional capacity to engage in different, locally appropriate development work. There is also the danger that the system for allocating finite national resources across different NGBs engenders competition, rather than cooperation, between them. Finally, fragmentation has been further engrained in the PE and school sport sector by the system through which funding and spending of the PE and Sport Premium are entirely delegated to individual primary schools. The increasing array of external and commercial providers of PE and school sport services, the limited coordination capacity and powers of local authorities or Active Partnerships, and the similar direction of wider education policies severely inhibit the government's own aspiration of "a joined-up sport and physical activity offer for young people" (Department for Education, Department for Digital, Culture, Media and Sport, and Department of Health and Social Care, 2019).

Summary

Sport policy in England has gone through a number of changes over the last 50 years. However, as outlined above, there are also a number of consistencies. In terms of organisation, sport in England remains complex – with NGBs, local authorities, Active Partnerships, and other civil society organisations all still playing varying roles in the provision and support of sport. There have been clearer divisions concerning grassroots sport and elite sport. The recent success of elite sport policy, in terms of medals at the summer Olympic and Paralympic Games at least, has come at a cost – both in terms of the culture developed in pursuit of that success and in terms of diverting funding away from grassroots provision. Alongside this, the 'wicked problems' in terms of a lack of participation in sport and physical activity among particular underrepresented groups – despite being the target of much sport policy over the last 50 years – persist. Furthermore, there has been a growing tendency for policymakers not only in government but also increasingly within NGBs to view sport in much broader terms, and this was reinforced with the publication of *Sporting Future*. Traditional, competitive sport (and the organisations that typically provide for such sport – namely NGBs) now needs to increasingly compete for public funding with a broader range of organisations, such as those in the sport-for-development movement, that have a much wider remit around physical activity and health more generally.

References

Bloyce, D., & Smith, A. (2010). *Sport Policy and Development. An Introduction.* London: Routledge.

Bostock, J., Crowther, P., Ridley-Duff, R., & Breese, R. (2018). No plan B: The achilles heel of high performance sport management. *European Sport Management Quarterly*, *18*(1), 25–46.

Chalip, L. (1995). Policy analysis in sport management. *Journal of Sport Management*, *9*(1), 1–13.

Coalter, F. (2013). *Game Plan* and *The Spirit Level*: The class ceiling and the limits of sports policy? *International Journal of Sport Policy and Politics*, *5*(1), 3–19.

De Bosscher, V., & van Bottenburg, M. (2011). Elite for all, all for elite? An assessment of the impact of sports development on elite sport success. In B. Houlihan & M. Green (eds.) *Routledge Handbook of Sports Development* (pp. 579–598). Abingdon: Routledge.

Department of Culture, Media and Sport (DCMS). (2008). *Playing to Win: A New Era for Sport*. London: DCMS.

Department for Culture, Media and Sport (DCMS)/ Strategy Unit (2002). *Game Plan: A Strategy for Delivering Government's Sport and Physical Activity Objectives*. London: DCMS/Strategy Unit.

Department for Education. (2013). National Curriculum in England: Primary Curriculum. Available at: https://www.gov.uk/government/uploads/system/

uploads/attachment_data/file/425601/PRIMARY_national_curriculum. pdf (accessed 21 October 2019).
Department for Education. (2019). Primary PE and Sport Premium Survey: Research Report. Available at: https://assets.publishing.service.gov.uk/government/uploads/system/uploads/attachment_data/file/816676/Primary_PE_and_Sport_Premium_Survey_research_report.pdf (accessed 21 October 2019).
Department for Education, Department for Digital, Culture, Media and Sport, and Department of Health and Social Care. (2019). School Sport and Activity Action Plan. Available at: https://assets.publishing.service.gov.uk/government/uploads/system/uploads/attachment_data/file/817093/School_sport_and_activity_action_plan.pdf (accessed 21 October 2019).
Department of National Heritage. (1995). *Sport: Raising the Game*. London: Department of National Heritage.
Green, M. (2007). Olympic glory or grassroots development?: Sport policy priorities in Australia, Canada and the United Kingdom, 1960–2006. *The International Journal of the History of Sport, 24*(7), 921–953.
Green, M. (2009). Non-governmental organisations in sports development. In V. Girginov (ed.) *Management of Sports Development* (pp. 103–122). Abingdon: Routledge.
Green, M., & Houlihan, B. (2005). *Elite Sport Development. Policy Learning and Political Priorities*. London: Routledge.
Griggs, G. (2016). Spending the Primary Physical Education and Sport Premium: A West Midlands case study. *Education 3–13, 44*(5), 547–555.
Griggs, G., & Randall, V. (2019). Primary physical education subject leadership: Along the road from in-house solutions to outsourcing. *Education 3–13, 47*(6), 664–677.
Grix, J., & Phillpots, L. (2011). Revisiting the 'governance narrative': 'Asymmetrical network governance' and the deviant case of the sports policy sector. *Public Policy and Administration, 26*(1), 3–19.
Hargreaves, J. (1986). *Sport, Power and Culture. A Social and Historical Analysis of Popular Sports in Britain*. New York: St Martin's Press.
Harris, J. (2018). The Case for Physical Education Becoming a Core Subject in the National Curriculum. Available at: http://www.afpe.org.uk/physical-education/wp-content/uploads/PE-Core-Subject-Paper-20-3-18.pdf (accessed 21 October 2019).
Harris, S., & Houlihan, B. (2016). Implementing the community sport legacy: The limits of partnerships, contracts and performance management. *European Sport Management Quarterly, 16*(4), 433–458.
Houlihan, B., & Green, M. (2006). The changing status of school sport and physical education: Explaining policy change. *Sport, Education and Society, 11*(1), 73–92.
Houlihan, B., & Green, M. (2009). Modernization and sport: The reform of Sport England and UK Sport. *Public Administration, 87*(3), 678–698.
Houlihan, B., & Lindsey, I. (2012). *Sport Policy in Britain*. London: Routledge.

Houlihan, B., & White, A. (2002). *The Politics of Sports Development: Development of Sport Or Development through Sport?* London: Routledge.

House of Lords. (2021). A National Plan for Sport, Health and Wellbeing: HL Paper 113 Report of Session 2021–22. Available at: https://publications.parliament.uk/pa/ld5802/ldselect/ldsportrec/113/11302.htm (accessed 26 September 2022).

House of Commons Library. (2019). Physical Education, Physical Activity and Sport in Schools. Available at: https://commonslibrary.parliament.uk/research-briefings/sn06836/ (accessed 31 March 2020).

HM Government. (2015). *Sporting Future: A New Strategy for an Active Nation.* London: HM Government.

Institute of Fiscal Studies. (2019). English Local Government Funding: Trends and Challenges in 2019 and Beyond. Available at: https://www.ifs.org.uk/uploads/English-local-government-funding-trends-and-challenges-in-2019-and-beyond-IFS-Report-166.pdf (accessed 26 May 2022).

Jones, L., & Green, K. (2017). Who teaches primary physical education? Change and transformation through the eyes of subject leaders. *Sport, Education and Society*, 22(6), 759–771.

Lindsey, I. (2020). Analysing policy change and continuity: Physical education and school sport policy in England since 2010. *Sport, Education, and Society*, 25(1), 27–42.

Lindsey, I., Metcalfe, S., Gemar, A., Alderman, J., & Armstrong, J. (2021). Simplistic policy, skewed consequences: Taking stock of English physical education, school sport and physical activity policy since 2013. *European Physical Education Review*, 27(2), 278–296.

Lovett, E., & Bloyce, D. (2017). What happened to the legacy from London 2012? A sociological analysis of the processes involved in preparing for a grassroots sporting legacy from London 2012 outside of the host city. *Sport in Society*, 20(11), 1625–1643.

Mori, K., Morgan, H., Parker, A., & Mackintosh, C. (*in press*). Examining the impact of austerity on community sport development workers and their professional environment. *Journal of Global Sport Management*. https://doi.org/10.1080/24704067.2021.1871803.

Sport England. (2004). *The Framework for Sport in England. Making England an Active and Successful Sporting Nation: A Vision for 2020.* London: Sport England.

Sport England. (2016). Towards an Active Nation. Available at: https://sportengland-production-files.s3.eu-west-2.amazonaws.com/s3fs-public/sport-england-towards-an-active-nation.pdf (accessed 5 January 2022).

Sport England. (2021). *Uniting the Movement.* London: Sport England.

Sport England. (2022). Active Lives Adult Survey: November 2020–21 Report. Available at: https://sportengland-production-files.s3.eu-west-2.amazonaws.com/s3fs-public/2022-04/Active%20Lives%20Adult%20Survey%20November%202020-21%20Report.pdf?VersionId=nPU_v3jFjwG8o_xnv62F-cKOdEiVmRWCb (accessed 19 May 2022).

Sports Council (1982). *Sport in the Community: The Next Ten Years.* London: Sports Council.

Thompson, A., Bloyce, D., & Mackintosh, C. (2021). "It is always going to change" – Examining the experiences of managing top-down changes by sport development officers working in national governing bodies of sport in England. *Managing Sport and Leisure*, 26(1–2), 60–79.

UK Sport. (n.d.). From Home 2 the Games. Available at: https://www.uksport.gov.uk/news/2021/06/02/from-home-2-the-games (accessed 10 April 2022).

Walker, C. M., & Hayton, J. W. (2018). An analysis of third sector sport organisations in an era of 'super-austerity'. *International Journal of Sport Policy and Politics*, 10(1), 43–61.

Widdop, P., King, N., Parnell, D., Cutts, D., & Millward, P. (2019). Austerity, policy and sport participation in England. In D. Parnell, P. Millward, P. Widdop, N. King, A May (eds.) *Sport Policy and Politics in an Era of Austerity* (pp. 6–23). London: Routledge.

Weed, M. (2016). Should we privilege sport for health? The comparative effectiveness of UK Government investment in sport as a public health intervention. *International Journal of Sport Policy and Politics*, 8(4), 559–576.

3 Sport Policy in Scotland

Grant Jarvie

Overview and structure of sport

Scotland often refers to itself and is referred to by others as a nation (Daiches, 1993). The Kingdom of Scotland emerged as an independent sovereign state in the 9th century, something that remained until the Union of the Parliaments of 1707. In 1999, the Scottish Parliament reconvened with significant but not fully devolved powers. Sport is a devolved operation but only in the sense that the devolved legal apparatus was provided under the Scotland Acts of 1998, 2012, and 2016. Scotland technically remains a sub-state of the United Kingdom (UK). It is not a fully fledged diplomatic actor, and it is not a fully independent, sovereign nation state with diplomatic staff, representation, and foreign embassies. International relations are reserved to Westminster under schedule 5 of the Scotland Act 1988. Scotland remains part of the United Kingdom apparatus through, for example, UK Sport and the Great Britain (GB) International Olympic Committee (Jarvie et al., 2017).

Scotland itself continues to evolve and change. According to the National Records of Scotland (NRS, 2022): 91% of Scotland's population lives in settlements and localities, which accounts for 2.3% of Scotland's total land area.[1] There were 514 settlements in Scotland in the mid-2020s. This is 5 fewer than 2016, due to some settlements merging or falling below the threshold of 500 people. The population of Scotland living in settlements in the mid-2020s was 4,974,670. The population living outside settlements was 491,330. The largest settlement in Scotland was Greater Glasgow with a population of 1,028,220. Nearly one in five people living in Scotland in mid-2020s lived in Greater Glasgow. Almost all of Glasgow and Dundee City's population lived in a settlement (99.8% in both). In contrast, less than a third of Na h-Eileanan Siar's (Outer Hebrides) population lived in a settlement (29.4%).

DOI: 10.4324/9781003241232-3

In terms of area, Scotland is about twice the size of the Netherlands and almost the same size as South Carolina in the United States of America (USA). In Scotland, there are 787 islands from which around 130 are inhabited and about 78,789 km^2 (30,420 miles^2). The newest city Dunfermline joins Glasgow, Edinburgh, Dundee, Aberdeen, Perth, Inverness, and Stirling, not to mention major towns including Paisley, East Kilbride, Livingston, Cumbernauld, Hamilton, Motherwell, Kirkcaldy, Ayr, and Kilmarnock to name but a few.

Scotland's wide and varied history, network, and influence highlight the potential of Scotland's sporting assets. Sport has played an important part in the making of Scotland and the lives of Scots. Several Acts of Parliament and Town Council Acts of the 15th and 16th centuries banned football, golf, and shinty. Football statistically is Scotland's number one sport although this was not always the case (Scottish Football Association, 2020). The world's oldest football, thought to date from the 1540s, was discovered in the rafters behind the ceiling of the Queen's Chamber at Stirling Castle. John Hope is credited with forming the first organised football club in Edinburgh in 1824. Queen's Park Football Club in Glasgow was the first Scottish club to form for the purpose of playing association football in 1867. Scottish football's financial dependency upon gate receipts, that is, people coming to watch the game, is higher than any other country in Europe (Scottish Football Association, 2020). In 1800, curling was the most popular game in the country (Haynes, 2014). A comparison of the Statistical Account of Scotland (1791–1799) and the New Statistical Account (1845) shows that there was more sport in Scotland around 1840 than there had been 50 years earlier. In shinty, golf, curling, Highland Games and Gatherings, and bowls, Scotland lays claim to have played such a large role that these sports are often claimed to be Scotland's cultural property (Jarvie & Burnett, 2000). Archery along with horse racing is the sport that can show the clearest line of tradition from the Middle Ages to the present day. The oldest sporting competition in Scotland is the Red House Race at Carnwath, near Lanark, a foot race for which there is firm evidence in 1456, which may be older.

The contemporary Scottish sporting landscape is complex (Scottish Government, 2019a, p. 1). The Scottish Government talks of this in the following terms:

> The sporting system is made up of different components that interact with each other. It is not a structure, an organisation or a process. The system adapts to its environment. So as the world

around sport changes, the system components and the way they interact evolves. In a changing world we need to be aware of what's happening and adapt when needed.

(Scottish Government, 2019b, p. 2)

The beginning of the 21st century has seen a renaissance in Scotland's sporting buildings and provision. In many cases, the investment of funding from the National Lottery, the Scottish Government, and the UK Government, primarily although not only, through the national sports agency, *Sportscotland*, has enabled projects that may not have been possible earlier. The Community Amateur Sports Club Scheme of 2002 enabled grassroots clubs to benefit from a range of tax reliefs. The policy of intentionally planning for and securing major sporting events (e.g., Commonwealth Games 2014, The Ryder Cup Golf 2014, UEFA 2020/2021 European Football Championships, The UCI Mountain Bike World Cup 2022, The World Athletic Indoor Championships 2024, The World Orienteering Championships 2024, and The Orkney Island Games 2025) has assisted Scotland's sporting profile and capability building. Sport is a cultural, social, and economic asset to Scotland whose potential has still to be fully realised. It is perhaps surprising that contemporary Scotland does not make more of sport as a tool for forging international and cultural relations.

Sport in Scotland is a devolved matter resulting from the powers delivered to Scotland through the Scotland Acts of 1998, 2006, and 2012 (Scottish Government, 2016; UK Government, 2021). The reality of sport in a devolved sub-state nation of the United Kingdom is not straightforward since Scottish sport also receives significant funding through the UK National Lottery system (Jarvie & Birnbacher, 2018). It is part of the UK sports system through UK Sport – the sport agency, whose strategic purpose is to "Lead high performance sport to enable extraordinary moments that enrich lives" (UK Sport, 2021, p. 11). Scottish sport is part of a changing international landscape. The UK left the European Union (EU) on 31 January 2020 following on from the UK Government and the EU agreeing to forge a deal on their future partnership. From 1st January 2021, this new relationship with the EU came into effect. There will be an impact upon many, if not all, of the areas of Scottish public life including changes to the Scottish sporting ecosystem from professional sports to grassroots and volunteering.

The advent of a global COVID-19 pandemic continues to leave its mark not just on Scottish sport. With the effects of the pandemic looking likely to be with us for some time, the entire sports ecosystem needs to be vigilant with potential threats to financial and business continuity arising from disrupted cash flows, legal and insurance challenges, and the possible impacts on longer-term attendance and engagement. The pandemic has only accelerated the realisation that Scottish sport in the future will have to work hard at maintaining, refreshing, and engaging with consumers in both old and new ways as sport in Scotland strives to move forward.

The impacts of COVID-19 on Scottish sport came in many forms although these were not unique to Scotland (Commonwealth Secretariat, 2020a, 2020b; Jarvie, 2021). They included the loss of connection with sport particularly for those on the margins of Scottish society; the cancellation of events; loss of sponsorship money; reduction in sports tourism; cash flow difficulties for clubs and organisations; unpaid workforces; decline in sports production and retail income; isolation; loneliness and mental health problems which impacted on Scottish para sports communities in particular; and overall declines in sport participation although some specific sports – mainly outdoor sports such as golf and tennis – experienced increases. Again, youth on the margins of society where sports engagement required access to facilities such as schools or sports centres witnessed a decline in participation, while individual sports such as running, Parkour, and general physical activity were less affected.

A crisis, however, often provides the potential for a level of creativity and innovation that, if capitalised upon, could help to shape the future in a way that is more resilient, more equitable, and more lucrative. It is important that Scottish sport continually reflect upon innovation and build in organisational capacity and capability for innovation. Football clubs, for example, invest in resources to advance and get an edge with on-field performances often at the expense of resources and innovation around off-field capabilities in relation to clubs, stadiums, fans, and potential fans. Both are needed. A primary lesson from the pandemic within and beyond Scotland remains that any preventive strategy must begin with planning and investment. Scotland needs to invest in community sport and sport for development as a strategy of prevention. Governments should plan for, fund, monitor, and evaluate community sport and sport for development as essential components of national population health strategies, but not just health. This chapter shall comment further on COVID-19 within the discussion on community sport.

The Scottish sporting landscape is wide and varied and supported at local, regional, and national levels by different entities. A wide range of organisations are involved in sports planning and delivery consisting of a range of partners including *sportscotland* (inclusive of the *sportscotland* Institute of Sport and three national centres (Glenmore, Cumbrae, Inverclyde – National Para Sports Centre operated through the *sportscotland* Trust Company)); in excess of 70 governing bodies of sport supporting individual sports; the private sector which includes companies delivering activity, facilities, and services to the sports market; NGOs, Voluntary Community, Third Sector not-for-profit organisations delivering sports activity beyond the traditional sports clubs – local authority (arm's length external organisations deliver a significant amount of the Scottish sporting effort); the Further and Higher Education sector which has a role in the delivery, production, and consumption of sport beyond college and university clubs since they also operate facilities and deliver activity for their local communities; the school estate, both public and private, which remains central to local provision; team Scotland, *sportscotland* (Institute of Sport), the British Olympic Committee, UK Sport, and the British Paralympic Committee which are integral to Scottish high performance sport; 32 local authorities which have a statutory obligation with regard to adequate sport and leisure provision; the UK Anti-Doping Agency, sports integrity units, and sport's governing bodies, key to the integrity of Scottish sport; EventScotland, Cities and Local Authorities, key to levering sporting events into Scotland and finally a range of representative bodies and members associations providing a range of single-issue and/or multi-issue forums and networks.

Despite its complexity and historical remits, the Scottish sporting landscape could be a lot more effective. A mapping exercise of the remits of key organisations would be a worthwhile exercise that would expose remit overlap and inefficiency. The opportunity to create an agreed common purpose around sport including key interventions and perhaps more importantly agreed messaging is getting better, but opportunities have still been missed.

Brief evolution of sport policy and politics

Scottish policy and politics are enabled through a complex set of arrangements including the Crown, commonly referred to as the Monarchy of the United Kingdom. The Scottish Government is the devolved government of Scotland, formed in 1999 as the Scottish Executive following the 1997 referendum on Scottish devolution. The elected legislature is the body of 129 Members of the Scottish Parliament (MSPs) commonly referred to as the Holyrood Parliament. Local Government in Scotland is organised through the 32 unitary local authorities consisting of councillors elected every five years. Sports policy and politics in a devolved Scotland is influenced by a wide range of stakeholders, with the primary ones being the Scottish Parliament through *sportscotland*, the 32 local authorities, and the UK Parliament through the UK Sports Council and the Department for Digital, Culture, Media and Sport (DCMS). Between 1999 and 2007, the Scottish Executive was led by a Scottish Labour Party and Scottish Liberal Democrat Party coalition. Since 2007, the Scottish Executive has been led by the Scottish National Party (SNP).

Let's get past the absurd politics question first: sport is inherently political. On any given day, sport is used as a tool to serve political functions and ends. There are times when sport can, does, and should lead by example. Yet will Scotland learn from other countries that place, for example, sport central in their thinking around diplomacy and national brand image. That is, take a sensible and rational approach in realising, beyond just rhetoric and media sound bites, that Scotland is a sporting nation, one that can harness sport and see it as a key driver in helping to deliver a wide range of outcomes beyond just sport.

The current strategic policy framework for Scottish Governing Bodies of Sport tends to be aligned with the following:

1 *Scotland's National Performance Framework* which sets out how Scotland can work together to achieve National Outcomes set by the Scottish Government (2022)
2 *Active Scotland Outcomes Framework* which outlines a shared vision of Scotland where more people are more active, more often (Scottish Government, 2018a)
3 *A More Active Scotland – Scotland's Physical Activity Delivery Plan* (Scottish Government, 2018b)
4 *Sport for Life* which is *sportscotland*'s corporate strategy focused upon developing an active Scotland where everyone benefits from sport (*Sportscotland*, 2019)
5 *Powering Success Inspiring Impact* which is UK Sport's strategic plan for 2021–2031 (UK Sport, 2021)

Scottish party-political manifestos can provide a guide to Scottish sports policy, politics, and priorities in public life. For a governing party it sets priorities, once elected it becomes a programme of work for ministers and a means of holding administrations to account. If required, a manifesto can be an important element in reaching a coalition deal, although such a deal has not been needed at Holyrood for 18 years. The last Scottish general election was held in 2021, and what was perhaps surprising was the degree of convergence or common ground for the next five years, except for the issues relating to independence. For those parties supporting independence, none of them commented upon how this would impact upon sport, or indeed the role of sport in an independent Scotland.

The main areas covered by the 2021 manifestos involving sport and physical activity included health and well-being, communities, equity, facilities, and participation and outdoor recreation. The Liberal Democrats said the most about sport and the Greens said the least. The Conservatives, Liberal Democrats, and Labour stated that they would support a 2030 FIFA World Cup Bid. The Greens stated that they would support a dedicated Minister for Sport. The SNP stated that by the end of the Parliament, 10% of the transport capital budget would be spent on walking, cycling, and wheeling. None of the parties referred to the impact of constitutional change on sport and recreation. The 2021 pledges offered by each of the political parties were as follows: Double the Scottish Government's investment in sport and active living to £100 million a year by the end of the Parliament (SNP); 10% of the transport capital budget to be spent on walking, cycling, and wheeling (SNP); £1 million to support more schools to open their facilities to the public during evenings and weekends (Conservatives); double *sportscotland*'s budget over the course of the next Parliament (Conservatives); develop a new Active Scotland Plan, enabling councils to reintegrate local services (Labour); appoint a Minister for Sport (Greens); back the UK's bid to host the 2030 World Cup and bid to hold the final in Scotland (Conservatives); extend opportunities for Gaelic sports (Liberal Democrats); appoint an Outdoor Recreation Champion (Liberal Democrats); establish an island travel scheme for teams and individuals to compete in national events (Liberal Democrats); and create a 'Fan Bank' to empower communities and groups and strengthen local decision-making by supporting communities to acquire a share or control of their local sports club (SNP) and participate in the UK-wide preparatory work for a 2030 Men's World Cup bid being funded by the UK Government (Liberal Democrats). Every £1 spent on sport generates £1.91 in health and social benefits, but none of the manifestos, according to the Institute for Fiscal Studies, were adequately costed.

It is equally important to consider what is not said and what could be said. Given Scotland's stated positive intentions on climate change, the Sustainable Development Goals (SDGs) and human rights, it is surprising that the political parties do not see sport as enabling outcomes in these areas. These are missed opportunities. What is perhaps even more surprising is that a nation that does not have control over foreign affairs and claims to be disadvantaged by Brexit has not maximised the benefits to be gained from grasping the potential of sport as a key component of culture to drive international relations, diplomacy, and soft power (Jarvie et al., 2017).

Other sporting nations have made the case for sport in a way that has enabled sport to gain traction, long-term funding, and profile across Government Ministries. Scottish sport must be better at making the case for sport outside of the sports world and beyond just the health portfolio in a way that releases funding for agreed outcomes across a much broader range of government budgets. Very little direct legislation concerning sport is passed by the Holyrood Parliament. The only Act of legislation, other than specific legislature for major sporting events, to be passed was the Offensive Behaviour at Football and Threatening Communications Scotland Act (2012). An Act that was subsequently repealed because it was seen as being ineffective.

Given the claim that Scotland is a sporting nation, it is perhaps surprising that specific sport-related policies, bills, charters, or Acts have been relatively few and far between. There is no Sports Act, there is no dedicated sports minister simply focusing upon sport, and the number of civil servants servicing sport is small, with one being solely dedicated to football. Policy concentration tends to be focused on active health outcomes, fan behaviour, and legislation that needs to be put in place for the hosting of specific major events. More than 90% of sport is delivered through local authorities or trusts, and yet sport is not a statutory provision within the Local Authority Act. The attention to sport in party-political manifestos is greater than other countries such as Canada, but, on the other hand, Scotland has no sports diplomacy strategy like Australia or Wales.

Elite sport

In 2024, it will be 100 years since Eric Liddell, the Scottish athlete and rugby player, gained Olympic success after refusing to run on a Sunday and ten years since the City of Glasgow hosted the Commonwealth Games. Scotland's women rugby players qualified for the Women's Rugby World Cup for the first time in 2022. The term 'world class' appears three times in *Sport for Life* – the national sports agencies' vision for sport in Scotland. World Class is referred to as one of six principles which are behind the vision. The Scottish sports system is talked of as a world-class sports system which makes the best use of

Scotland's assets and adapts to change. Performance sport is supported through the Scottish Institute of Sport – a directorate of *sportscotland*, the national sports agency. World class is used to describe the agencies approach to everything it does. This means doing everything to the highest possible standard while seeking to continuously improve.

The main constituents of the Scottish World Class system are the national sports agencies for Scotland and the UK, the national sports governing bodies, Commonwealth Games Scotland, the university sector, and local authorities. Scotland has no Olympic Committee and is part of the Great Britain and Northern Ireland Olympic Association.

Scottish athletes made up about 10% of Team GB that went to the Tokyo 2020 (+1) Olympic Games. Fifty-three Scottish athletes were part of Team GB (32 female and 21 male). They returned from the Tokyo 2020 (+1) Olympic Games with a record medal total of 14 including 3 gold, 8 silver, and 3 bronze. The overall total surpasses the 13 medals won by Scottish athletes at both the London and Rio Olympic Games. Scottish athletes made up more than a third of the 50-strong British team that headed to the Beijing 2022 Winter Olympic Games. The 19 Scots included curler Eve Muirhead, who competed in her fourth Olympic Games and secured her first Olympic gold medal. Paralympics GB sent its biggest team to a Paralympic Winter Games since Lillehammer 1994 with 25 athletes making the team. There were 14 Scottish athletes in the team making up 56% of the team, the largest Scottish contingent ever.

The Commonwealth Games is the only multi-sport event where Scotland competes as a nation. From their debut in the 1930 Commonwealth Games in Hamilton, Canada, Scotland was represented by 15 athletes in 1930 and the county has taken part in every Commonwealth Games since then (one of only six nations to do so, the others being Australia, Canada, England, New Zealand, and Wales). In a world where sport is increasingly recognised as a soft power asset, sporting influence matters, and nations often ask themselves how many people they should have in positions of power and influence in world sport. Dame Louise Martin, President of the Commonwealth Games Federation, is one such Scot, with Kate Caithness, Katherine Grainger, Craig Reedie, and Alex Ferguson being a few of the other Scottish sporting influencers who hold or who have recently held key posts.

A well-funded sports system with a commitment to both high performance and sport for all is essential to an equitable and vibrant Scotland but remains work in progress. A well-funded state-led sports system could be the right approach. However, one of the consequences of the neoliberal assaults on the ideals and programmes of the welfare state is that it is very difficult for governments, whether they be Scottish or British, to mount ambitious high-quality social programmes for sport. Many in Scotland send their kids to private fitness clubs, the private sector schools have stronger sports programmes, and successive governments have shied away from the levels of taxation or refused to endorse the policy reforms that would help to provide similar opportunities for every youth and adult. A study of British medal winners at Tokyo 2020 (+1) Olympics found 35% were educated privately for at least some of their secondary schooling up to 16 (Belger, 2021). The findings suggest progress in closing the state-private school gap has gone into reverse. Thirty-two percent of British medal winners in Rio in 2016 were privately educated. While the social composition of Scotland's world-class international sports teams is more democratic than that of the UK or Great Britain, sport in Scotland remains a middle-class affair.

Sport for all remains an aspiration (Kidd, 2021). A challenge for the sport sector is to understand and interpret changes in the law, policy, and politics into operational and strategic actions around equalities. Leadership positions and boards in Scottish sport are almost entirely white. The cost of accessing sport and facilities remains a significant barrier, with sport being available to those from wealthier backgrounds. Many sports still have a gender imbalance, and while there is much in Scottish sport to be proud of, Scotland does not yet have a world-class sports system that is equitable, fair, and just.

Participation and community sport

At the local level, Scotland's 32 local authorities manage most sports facilities including both community-based and school-based facilities. Scotland's local authorities work in partnership with some 26 trusts responsible for some 1,200 facilities, 18,000 staff, and over 12,000 volunteers. Some 95% of sport in Scotland is delivered at local levels through local authorities and trusts (COSLA, 2021). It is a myth to assert that all 26 trusts and 32 local authorities operate on the same model since they all have a different scale, different local challenges and opportunities, and different political leaders at a local authority level. They have in common central government cuts to local budgets and the need to resource both statutory and non-statutory levels of provision.

The Local Government and Planning Scotland Act 1982 states that with certain exceptions a local authority shall ensure that there is *adequate* provision of facilities for the inhabitants of the area for recreational, sporting, cultural, and social activities. After the statutory expenditure on health and social care and education is allocated, more than 50%, the discretionary expenditure for other areas of budget remains problematic and difficult to plan for and with. There is no mechanism for defining what adequate provision for sport means, is, or should be. It is different for different local authorities. There is a need for a new round of advocacy that asserts the right of sport for all and shifts sport and leisure provision from that of being adequate to statutory. Furthermore, there are no consistent Scottish mechanisms to review adequate provision of sport across 32 local authority areas. Local authority funding remains highly centralised and controlled from the Scottish Parliament and the places where most sports provision in Scotland happens, that is, local authorities. Sport is not a priority, but it should be more of a priority.

The 2018 report on *Sport for Everyone* noted that public funding of sport and physical recreation comes from *sportscotland* – the national sports agency and local authorities (*sportscotland*, 2018). At the time, funding stood at around £500 million per year, with local authorities providing around £400 million of this. *Sportscotland*'s total expenditure was £64 million in 2021–2022, falling to £63.6 million in 2022–2023. Direct government revenue funding for sport in Scotland, through *sportscotland*, equated to £34.7 million in 2022–2023 out of a health and social care budget of £18 billion. The health and social care budget equates to about 44% of the Scottish total budget. Direct government revenue funding for sport in 2021–2022 equated to £35.4 million (*sportscotland*, 2022). In 2009–2010, the budget allocation to sports was £37.1 million, while in 2018–2019, it was £34.9 million (Jarvie & Birnbacher, 2018).

The onset of the COVID-19 pandemic since March 2020 has impacted upon local Scottish sport and recreation provision. COVID-19 exposed the underfunding of community sport and physical education, which resulted in the sector being unable to optimise community sport as a significant resource of resilience for country populations. Some countries were slow to release restrictions on, for example, outdoor recreations/sports where benefits outweighed the risks. While participation in some outdoor sports such as golf and tennis increased in general, participation in sport and physical activity fell significantly because of the pandemic; a trend that had a likely severe impact on mental health and exacerbated an already low participation rate amongst girls, women, and para sport communities.

Recovery from the pandemic was always going to be difficult. Compound the impact of the pandemic, with the cost-of-living crisis fuelled by Brexit and the War in Ukraine and real-term cuts of local authority budgets, and we have a combination of factors that continue to hit Scottish society hard. The Convention of Scottish Local Authorities (COSLA) has warned that local authorities face £251 million real-term cuts in 2022, followed by a further £120 million in 2023 (Grant, 2002, p. 5). Levels of social cohesion have got worse since the pandemic. There have been changes in the availability and functions of public services. According to Scottish Government figures, those in the most deprived areas are more likely to say that their neighbourhood has got worse (33%) compared with 12% in the least deprived area (McLaughlin, 2022, p. 24). As of May 2022, community centres, leisure centres, social work services, and sport and exercise groups for old and young have not retuned to pre-COVID levels, many remain closed. If people cannot come together, then they cannot be communities in the making.

The COVID-19 pandemic created a human crisis of unprecedented scale, which internationally and disproportionately impacted one billion people with disabilities. The social inequality exacerbated by the pandemic has drawn increased attention to the medical and social determinants of health in Scotland. In keeping with the 2030 Sustainable Development Goals, a social determinant lens on building back better from COVID-19 requires (1) an equity lens to ensure that no one is left behind; (2) a return to pre-COVID or higher levels of involvement in community sport as a basis for further progress; (3) a new round of local, regional, and national advocacy and commitment by community groups to sport and related areas as an enabler of not just mental health outcomes; and (4) an urgent need to redesign the social contract.

Physical education and school sport

In 2013, *sportscotland* carried out an audit of the Scottish school estate to ascertain answers to three key questions (*sportscotland*, 2013): What sports facilities exist within the school estate? What sports facilities are available for use within the school estate? What is the current use of these facilities for sport? Improving access to the school estate was seen as one of the key success measures in the 2011–2015 corporate plan. The key findings at the time were:

- There were a wide range of sports facilities in Scotland's 2,102 primary schools and 371 secondary schools.
  - 79% of these facilities in primary schools were available for community use.

- 98% of these facilities in secondary schools were available for community use.
- 35% of available indoor space was used during term time (17% during school holidays).
- 19% of available outdoor space was used during term time (11% during school holidays).
- That use of secondary schools was significantly higher than that of primary schools.
- 61% of available indoor space in secondary schools was used during term time (43% during school holidays).
- 40% of available outdoor space in secondary schools was used during term time (28% during school holidays).
- For primary schools, two thirds (66%) of the use is by regular lets and a third (32%) is casual use.
- For secondary schools, 73% of the use is by regular lets and 26% is casual use.

The core conclusions to be drawn from the report were that there are a wide range of facilities for sport within the school estate and a wide range of sports taking place in these facilities. Most of the school estate was available for public use during both term time and school holidays. Most of the indoor space in secondary schools is used by the community, but there is scope to increase use across the entire estate.

Seventy percent of Scotland's Olympic medal winners at the London 2012 Olympics went to state schools. As indicated earlier, the *schools weekly* analysis of Tokyo 2020, which included Scottish athletes, concluded that 35% of British medal winners at Tokyo were educated privately for at least some of their secondary schooling up to 16 (Belger, 2021).

In 2017, Scottish Labour argued that more than 1,000 schools have no outdoor sports facilities. It claimed the figures provided to it by *sportscotland* show not enough is being invested by the Scottish government. A total of 1,040 schools were recorded as having no outdoor facilities. The schools without outdoor facilities included four in ten primary schools and three quarters of schools for those with additional support needs (BBC, 2017).

The approach to physical education and physical activity is very much a whole school approach, something that is internationally recognised (COSLA, 2021). This involves prioritising regular, high-quality, physical education classes; providing suitable physical environments and resources to support structured and unstructured physical activity throughout the day (e.g., play and recreation before, during and after school); supporting active travel to school programmes; and enabling these actions through supportive school policies and by engaging staff, students, parents, and the wider community (COSLA, 2021). This approach provides maximal opportunities for school-based physical activity participation, particularly given that children spend more time in schools than in any other venue away from home and can also apply to nurseries.

Taking a rights-based approach goes hand in hand with education and children's services; health and social care; strong, safe, and sustainable communities and local economies; inclusive growth; and the environment (Harvey, 2020). The proposed United Nations Convention on the Rights of the Child (UNCRC) (Incorporation) (Scotland) Bill21 seeks to enshrine in the UNCRC in Scots law, making it unlawful for public authorities to act incompatibly with the incorporated UNCRC requirements, giving children, young people, and their representatives the power to enforce their rights (COSLA, 2021). Article 31, the Right to Play, includes the right of the child to engage in play and recreational activities appropriate to their age and culture, while Article 24 focuses on the Right to Health and Health Services. Whilst the *International Charter of Physical Education, Physical Activity and Sport* states that physical education, and sport is a fundamental right for all, a rights-based approach to physical education, physical activity, and sport remains work in progress in Scotland (COSLA, 2021). While the Scottish Parliament backed respective bills which attempted to enshrine treaties on children's rights and local government in Scots law – prior to the 2017 Holyrood parliamentary elections, Judges at the Supreme Court ruled that provisions in two bills passed by MSPs were beyond Holyrood's powers (BBC, 2021).

Direct and indirect legislative requirements exist relating to sport and recreation provision with those indirect interventions relating to equalities, child protection, fairer Scotland, human rights, and public sector provision. It would be a mistaken to suggest that a single model exists.

Sport development programmes and policies

Universal access to sport remains a work in progress, and while social characteristics are protected under the provision of the Equalities Act, social class, poverty, and geography are still significant barriers to sport in Scotland that should not be ignored. Sport in Scotland is a complex landscape. The responsibility for sport is shared across a range of organisations at both national and local levels. If Scotland is going to maximise the benefit of sport, then it is paramount that an enlarged agreed common ground and purpose needs to be forthcoming. Scotland has given a lot to the world of sport, but it also needs to consider further embracing opportunities that are presented. Scottish society is changing, and sport needs to adapt with it and be more representative of it.

The potential for Scotland to lead on issues such as sport and human rights; sport and the sustainable development goals, and maximise the soft power potential of Scottish sport is very real but has yet to be fully realised. Scotland has a lot to offer. Both Scotland and the Scottish sports industry could further advance Scotland's international interests by grasping sport's ability to engage with other governments and cities and open the door not just for business but for cultural exchanges and messaging. Sport can help to advance Scotland's international connectivity, soft power, and para-diplomatic networks. The promise of removing barriers to youth sport for those who have experienced or are experiencing poverty in Scotland requires greater devolved support from the state so that the local promise of local authority aspirations for sport and recreation can be fully realised.

Unlike Canada, neither Scotland nor the UK has dedicated social science sports research funding streams, which means the evidence base for sport in comparison with other areas is another inequality gap that needs closing. The ability of Scottish sport to attract philanthropy as a significant additional income stream to support social outcomes is in its infancy, but in the spirit of Andrew Carnegie worth developing. It could be the third main income stream for Scottish sport, which in turn could learn a lot from the university sector on how to do this. Scotland has given a lot to the world of sport, but it also needs to consider further embracing opportunities that are currently presented.

As indicated earlier, local authorities have a statutory responsibility to provide *adequate f*acilities for the inhabitants of their area for recreational, sporting, cultural, and social activities, but this is not statutory and open to choice. This remains *a highly problematic situation* that is made worse during times of budgetary constraint. The noise about Scotland being a sporting nation is rarely matched in terms of state sporting finances nor obligations to the rest of the world through sport. Scotland does not maximise the opportunity given to it through sport having an international sporting mandate.

Challenges and barriers to sport development

Broader challenges for sport, physical activity, and physical education in Scotland stem mainly from the political economy of Scotland and the ongoing constitutional debate; a context which contributes to the creation of myth, instability, and public resources that could be used for sport, physical activity, and physical education being used for other purposes. Scotland proudly claims to be a sporting nation but rarely are the necessary resources available to enable the aspiration. Culturally sport is a valued cultural asset. Football is by far the most popular sport with gate receipts contributing to a higher ratio of football funding than anywhere else in Europe. In October 2022, Scotland became the world's first Daily Mile Nation with all 32 local authorities becoming involved. There is much to be proud of, but structural challenges and tensions exist.

Politically and economically the argument for sport has still to be won. This remains the case, whatever the outcome of the constitutional debate. No dedicated portfolio or Minister for Sport and related areas exists. This matters when it comes to arguing for resources at the cabinet level. The provision of sport and recreation is not a statutory provision at the local authority level. Direct government expenditure on sport although increasing remains low in comparison with other nations, never mind the aspiration goal of being politically and economically a sporting nation. As indicated above, their remains an alarming social divide in terms of both social class and regional inequality; these areas that are not adequately covered within the provisions of the Equalities Act. The number of official Olympic training centres within Scotland remains low. Top slicing from other portfolios which sport delivers on is not forthcoming. The last time the top slicing from other budgets made a difference was in the creation of the active school sport coordinators programme in the 1990s. The current immigration debate threatens to impact upon international student numbers at Scotland's universities, which would have an indirect impact upon university and college funding and the resources available for sport, physical activity, and physical education facilitated through these institutions.

The key message from this brief overview of some of the broader challenges facing Scottish sport, at the time of writing, is that the argument for sport has still to be won politically and economically. Scottish sport is not divorced from the broader political economy of Scotland and the United Kingdom, and both governments could and should do more to alleviate the fear that sport, physical activity, and physical education do not matter in terms of priorities.

Summary

Scottish sport has travelled a long way since the kirk session records of Glasgow wrote of schynnie in 1589 or Bishop Hamilton of St Andrews in 1552 allocated the town's western links for golf, football, shooting, and all games. Scotland as a country continues to change. If Scotland is to capitalise on the current UN sporting mandate that sport is provided with through the 2030 sustainable development goals, then it needs to be recognised and funded as the real social, cultural, and economic asset that it is and could be to Scotland.

There are several key messages that can be taken from this review of sport in Scotland. First, the structure of the Scottish sporting landscape is complex, and an agreed common purpose across a wide range of stakeholders is a challenge, but it would help Scotland if it were to speak only with one voice. Second, rather than developing and prioritising coherent joined up policies on how sport can advance sporting and non-sporting outcomes, most political parties have tended to focus upon local delivery models through trusts and the tax status of arm's length bodies rather than top sliced intentionally planned programmes and policies that can deliver against a wide range of non-sporting outcomes. The Active Schools sports programme emerged in the 1970s, but this is the last time a top slice from across budget portfolios has funded programmes. Perhaps it is time for more of this. Third, some 90% of sport is provided publicly through local authorities whose budgets have been centrally controlled and repeatedly cut for the past 13 or 14 years except for 2014 and the Commonwealth Games. The 2021 budget outturn for culture and recreation services – including sport, was £557 million compared to £602 million in 2013 (Scottish Government, 2021). Fourth, sport should matter to Scotland in the global plural 21st century not simply because nations can create influence and status within sport but more importantly through sport. Sports diplomacy and cultural relations building are not necessarily axiomatic with the state, and smaller nations and sub-states need to be bolder and innovative in how they attract trade, tourists, and publics. Marrying tried and tested soft power means to Scotland's powerful brand, culture, and values is one way of doing this. Scotland could do better. One final point to conclude would be to acknowledge that some of the local and international challenges that Scotland and the world faces are systemic and that sport as a tool can only do so much. Sport should not be expected to solve the problems of the world, but it should get more recognition than it does for what it has done internationally and locally. This is also the case for Scotland and what sport has done and can do for Scotland and its place in the world.

Note

1 NRS uses information about postcodes (some 140,000 in Scotland) to define "settlements" and "localities" to approximate built-up areas. Settlements are defined as groups of adjacent, densely populated postcode areas that have a combined population of 500 people or more. Some settlements are divided into localities to reflect the areas that are more easily identifiable as the towns and cities of Scotland.

References

BBC (2017). 'No outdoor sport' at over 1,000 Scottish schools. *BBC News*, 3 January. https://www.bbc.co.uk/news/uk-scotland-scotland-politics-38488304 [accessed 22 May 2022].

BBC (2021) Supreme court upholds challenges to two Holyrood Bills. *BBC News*, 6 October. https://www.bbc.co.uk/news/uk-scotland-scotland-politics-58794698 [accessed 22 February 2023].

Belger, T. (2021). Private schools extend Olympic medal lead but Eton stumbles. *Schools Week*, 6 April.

Commonwealth Secretariat. (2020a). A special report on sport and physical activity and Covid-19: The implications of COVID-19 for community sport and sport for development. *Commonwealth Moves* 2020 January. Commonwealth Secretariat.

Commonwealth Secretariat. (2020b). A special report on sport and physical activity and Covid-19: Resourcing the sustainability and recovery of the sport sector during the coronavirus pandemic. *Commonwealth Moves* 2020 February. Commonwealth Secretariat.

COSLA. (2021). The positive contribution of physical activity and sport to Scotland. https://www.cosla.gov.uk/__data/assets/pdf_file/0021/24942/COSLA-PA-Contribution-Briefing-V8.pdf [accessed 20 October 2022].

Daiches, D. (1993). *A companion to Scottish culture*. Polygon Press.

Grant, A. (2022). Vital council services face cuts unless funding improves. *Scotland on Sunday*, 22 May, p. 5.

Harvey, M. (2020). *Return to play: Sport's COVID-19 responses need to include the human rights of children and youth*. Geneva: Centre for Sport and Human Rights

Haynes, H. (2014). *Scotland's sporting buildings*. Historic Scotland.

Jarvie, G. (2021). Sport, covid recovery and building back better: Some observations. *Sport Matters* 2021 January. https://www.blogs.hss.ed.ac.uk/sport-matters/2021/01/31/sport-covid-recovery-and-building-back-better-some-observations/ [accessed 21 October 2022].

Jarvie, G., Murray, S., & Macdonald, S. (2017). Promoting Scotland, diplomacy and influence through sport. *Scottish Affairs*, 26(1), 1–22.

Jarvie, G., & Birnbacher, D. (2018). Sport, austerity or choice: An analysis of direct government expenditure on sport. *Scottish Affairs*, 27(2), 189–214.

Jarvie, G., & Burnett, J. (2000). *Sport, Scotland and the Scots*. Tuckwell Press.

Kidd, B. (2021). *A runner's journey*. University of Toronto Press.

McLaughlin, M. (2022). After the pandemic, a new struggle. *Scotland on Sunday*, 22 May, pp. 23–25.

National Records of Scotland. (2022). *Mid-year population estimates*. https://www.nrscotland.gov.uk/statistics-and-data/statistics/statistics-by-theme/population/population-estimates/mid-year-population-estimates [accessed 20 October 2022].

Scottish Football Association. (2020). The value of football. UEFA 2020. https://www.scottishfa.co.uk/football-development/value-of-football/ [accessed 20 October 2022].

Scottish Government. (2016). *Scotland Acts 2012 and 2016 implementation: Annual reports*. Scottish Government. https://www.gov.scot/publications/fourth-annual-report-implementation-scotland-act-2016-eighth-annual-report-implementation-operation-part-3-financial-provisions-scotland-act-2012/ [accessed 20 October 2022].

Scottish Government. (2018a). *Active Scotland outcome framework*. Scottish Government. https://www.gov.scot/publications/active-scotland-delivery-plan/pages/5/ [accessed 19 October 2022].

Scottish Government. (2018b). *A more active Scotland*. Scottish Government. https://www.gov.scot/binaries/content/documents/govscot/publications/strategy-plan/2018/07/active-scotland-delivery-plan/documents/00537494-pdf/00537494-pdf/govscot%3Adocument/00537494.pdf [accessed 19 October 2022].

Scottish Government. (2019a). *The Jarvie report on the Scottish sporting landscape*. Scottish Government Publications.

Scottish Government. (2019b). *Scottish government response to the recommendations of the Jarvie report on the Scottish sporting landscape*. Scottish Government Publications.

Scottish Government. (2021). *Scottish budget 2022–23*. Scottish Government Publications.

Scottish Government. (2022). *National performance framework 2022*. Scottish Government. https://nationalperformance.gov.scot/ [accessed 19 October 2022].

Sportscotland. (2013). *School estate audit: Sports facilities in schools*. Sportscotland.

Sportscotland. (2018). *Evaluation of sportscotland supported activity 2018*. Sportscotland.

Sportscotand. (2019). *Sport for life: A vision for sport in Scotland*. Sportscotland.

Sportscotland. (2022). *Playing our part 2022*. Sportscotland. https://sportscotland.org.uk/about-us/playing-our-part-2022/ [accessed 20 October 2022].
UK Sport. (2021). *United Kingdom strategic plan for sport 2021–2031*. Department of Culture, Media and Sport.
United Kingdom Government. (2018). *The Scotland Act 1998*. Legislation Government UK. https://www.legislation.gov.uk/ukpga/1998/46/contents [accessed 20 October 2022].

4 Sport Policy in Wales

Nicola Bolton

Overview and structure of sport

Wales is a country of 3.1 million people (ONS, 2022), with the highest population densities found in the towns and cities in South and North Wales as well as the traditional industrial coal-mining areas of the South Wales Valleys and North East Wales. The remaining population is found mostly in small towns and villages dispersed across the country. Cardiff is the capital city with a population of 362,400 (ONS, 2022), and with its own national language, Wales is steeped in a strong cultural heritage. It has an outstanding natural landscape with three national parks, five Areas of Outstanding Natural Beauty, and 1,400 km of coastline, which forms Wales' Coastal Path.

Sport is important to Wales. Although there has not been a major multi-sport event since the British Empire and Commonwealth Games held in Cardiff in 1958, significant international competitions have been held including 1999 Rugby World Cup, six FA Cup football finals, 2009 Ashes Test, 2010 Ryder Cup, 2017 UEFA Champions League football finals, 2017 ICC Champions Trophy and IT20 cricket, 2018 Volvo Ocean Race, and 2019 Homeless World Cup. There have been other notable sporting developments such as the Cardiff Half Marathon, which started in 2003 with 1,500 runners and is now the UK's second largest half marathon with over 25,000 runners. Wales's sporting heritage is complemented by several professional sports including football, rugby union, cricket, golf, and ice hockey. Has an increasingly commercial base in which the pre-pandemic value of sport to the Welsh economy had grown with consumers spending £1.26 billion, sport-related GVA stood at £1.195 billion and over 30,000 (full-time equivalent) sport-related jobs (Davies & Kokolakakis, 2018).

The formal development of sport policy can be traced back to the establishment of the Sports Council for Wales[1] on the 4th February in

DOI: 10.4324/9781003241232-4

1972 under Royal Charter, with the objectives of fostering the knowledge and practice of sport and physical recreation among the public at large in Wales and the provision of sports facilities (Sport Wales, 2022a). Since then, the objectives of participation, performance, facility development, and information have provided the organising mechanisms for the development of sport in Wales.

Sport has many stakeholders, with the traditional partners being viewed as the National Governing Bodies of Sport (NGBs) and Local Authorities (LAs). There are over 60 officially recognised NGBs in Wales (Sport Wales, 2022b), with only a small proportion of them funded by Sport Wales. However, all NGBs are influenced and impacted by Sport Wales's policies, and those that receive funding must achieve pre-agreed performance targets. At the community level, sport is organised through 22 single unitary LAs which in 1996 replaced 8 county councils and 37 district councils. Under the pre-1996 two-tier system, district councils had responsibility for leisure services and county councils had responsibility for education, and both levels of local government carried significant national influence in resourcing and shaping community sport policy (Robinson, 2004). Since 1996, there have been multiple internal re-organisations within Welsh LAs which have led to sport and leisure moving into larger directorates such as education, economic development, regeneration, or social care. The Welsh Government is the principal stakeholder and works closely with Public Health Wales (PHW) and Natural Resources Wales (NRW). Other important national organisations include the Welsh Sports Association, Disability Sport Wales, the Urdd, and StreetGames.

Brief evolution of sport policy and politics

The Royal Charter established Sport Wales as a separate and independent organisation, although it could be argued that during its first years Sports Wales's broad policy direction was similar to that found in England. Wales's first national ten-year strategy, *Changing Times: Changing Needs*, was launched in 1986 (Sports Council for Wales, 1986), but such was the pace of change that a revised strategy *Changing Times: Changing Needs, A Strategy Review* was published within three years (Sports Council for Wales, 1989), reflecting new legislation on marketisation and privatisation (e.g., Education Reform Act and Compulsory Competitive Tendering). These two strategies reflected the wider UK sporting policy landscape as outlined by Houlihan and White (2002) and were greatly influenced by Westminster politics. Policy differences with England were nuanced and could be categorised as 'context specific' (reflecting Wales's particular characteristics) and 'presentation specific' (e.g., the use of school facilities was called 'optimum use' in Wales rather than 'dual use', as it was known in England), which lends some weight to a perception of policy in Wales being largely an extension of sport development in England (Mackintosh, 2021).

Prior to devolution in the late 1990s, Sport Wales reported to the Secretary of State for Wales and the Welsh Office, and whilst operating independently from the Sports Council (GB), it has, until recently (Lindsey & Houlihan, 2013; Mackintosh, 2021), been treated as a branch of that organisation (Houlihan & White, 2002; Collins, 2010). This reflected the dominance of Westminster control over legislation and education and health policy.

After the 1997 general election, Labour quickly held referendums on devolution for Scotland and Wales. On the 18th September 1997, Wales voted 'yes' to devolution albeit by a very small majority of 50.3% (a margin of just 6,721 votes), with the then Secretary of State for Wales, Ron Davies, suggesting that Welsh devolution was "a process, not an event" (Torrance, 2022, p. 4). The process has so far been characterised by four distinct phases: from the Government of Wales Act 1998, which transferred the existing basic powers that resided with the Welsh Office to the National Assembly for Wales,[2] to the Wales Act 2017 when a model based on reserved powers was agreed alongside the establishment of the Senedd Cymru (Welsh Parliament) in 2020. In spite of calls to increase the number of Senedd Members, it has remained at 60 throughout, comprising 40 constituency members and 20 regional members (Torrance, 2022). The Welsh Assembly/Parliament is elected using the D'Hondt proportional method, and whilst Labour has been the largest party in all six elections, it has never won an outright majority.

The closeness of the devolution vote, together with its restricted policymaking powers and administrative capacity, resulted in the National Assembly for Wales looking to legitimise its role by producing distinctive policies and programmes (Tewdwr-Jones, 2001). Poverty and social deprivation were high on the agenda, as was health (Drakeford, 2006), and early policy responses (Murphy et al., 2017) were seen as seeking to tackle evident social and economic inequalities.

Initially, sport found itself in the shadows with no minister for sport in the first cabinet. This was rectified a year later in 2000, when Labour went into coalition with the Liberal Democrats and the then Minister for Culture, Sport and the Welsh Language (2000–2003) launched an all-encompassing strategy albeit heavily weighted to culture and heritage with only light reference to sport. As devolution gathered pace, however, the spotlight turned towards sport and physical activity, and since 2000, there has been a raft of strategies and policies. For ease of reference, these are presented in Table 4.1 and will be referred to under the relevant sections in this chapter. Notably, all of the documents listed in Table 4.1 have been produced *either* by Sport Wales *or* by the Welsh Government, but never *jointly*, and whilst this legitimately reflects the 'arms length' nature of Sport Wales from the Welsh Government, it may also be symptomatic of the way in which sport policy has been pulled in different directions, which has impeded the voice and impact of sport in Wales.

An early manifestation of the Welsh Government's intent to pursue a distinctive policy agenda was the 2005 "bonfire of the quangos" (Morgan & Upton, 2005, p. 2). Ministers argued that there were too many separate organisations which if brought under direct control would lead to service improvements and be more responsive to user needs. Sport Wales found itself embroiled in this issue with its then Chair describing the relationship with Government as one in which the "arms are getting shorter" (Morgan & Upton, 2005, p. 20). The First Minister of Wales, Rhodri Morgan announced in July that the Wales Tourist Board, the Welsh Development Agency, and Education and Learning Wales would be abolished and that a further 13

Table 4.1 Strategy and Policy Impacting on the Development of Sport in Wales (1997–2022)

Date	Sport Wales	Welsh Government
1997	Putting Young People First: A Strategy for Sport	
2005		Climbing Higher: The Welsh Assembly Strategy for Sport and Physical Activity
2006		Climbing Higher: Next Steps
2009		Creating an Active Wales
2010	Coaching Strategy 2010–2016 Elite Sport Strategy 2010–2016	Event Wales: A Major Events Strategy for Wales 2010–2020
2011	A Vision for Sport in Wales	Welsh Language (Wales) Measure 2011
2012	Community Sport Strategy Child Poverty Strategy	The Schools and Physical Activity Task and Finish Group convened by Minister for Housing, Regeneration and Heritage and Minister for Education and Skills

(*Continued*)

Table 4.1 (Continued)

Date	Sport Wales	Welsh Government
2013	Strategic Equality Plan 2012–2016	
2014		Communities, Equality and Local Government Committee: Inquiry into Participation Levels in Sport
2015	Elite Sport Strategy Governance and Leadership Framework	The Well-Being of Future Generations (Wales) Act 2015
2016	Facilities for Future Generations: A Blueprint for Sport and Active Recreation in Wales Strategic Equality Plan 2016–2020	Summary of Wales 2026 Commonwealth Games Feasibility Study
2017	Strategic Equality Action Plan 2016–2017	Sport Wales Review: An Independent Report for the Minister for Social Services and Public Heath
2018	Vision for Sport in Wales: Towards as Active Nation Strategy for Sport Wales	
2019	Governance and Leadership Framework for Wales	Healthy Weight: Healthy Wales Strategy
2022		The National Events Strategy for Wales 2022 to 2030 Levelling the Playing Field: A Report on the Participation in Sport and Physical Activity in Disadvantaged Areas – Welsh Parliament

organisations, including Sport Wales, were intended to be absorbed into the Government at a later date. Following consultation, however, Sport Wales (along with the Arts Council of Wales) retained its organisational identity albeit with some attempt to reduce its powers.

Sport was further propelled into the Welsh Government's policy-making arena with the launch of *Climbing Higher* (Welsh Assembly Government, 2005, 2006), a 20-year strategy for sport and physical activity in Wales. This far-reaching and ambitious strategy was developed for multiple stakeholders but surprisingly made little or no reference to Sport Wales and its strategy (Sports Council for Wales, 1997). With 19 aims, *Climbing Higher* involved multiple stakeholders, and thus, its implementation proved challenging and led to establishing a multi-agency Physical Activity Ministerial Advisory Group in 2009 (Welsh Assembly Government, 2009). Concomitant to this overarching strategy, the Welsh Government mirrored other home nations in showing an interest in elite sport and major sporting events. Following an independent review, Sport Wales produced its first elite sport strategy (Sport Wales, 2010b), which was updated in 2015 (Sport Wales, 2015a). Under the auspices of economic development, two event strategies (Welsh Assembly Government, 2010; Welsh Government, 2022) were published, and a feasibility study to host the 2026 Commonwealth Games (Welsh Government, 2016) was produced – the latter not progressing to a full bid because while technically possible, the costs were felt to be too great.

Since devolution, Sport Wales has also prepared and launched its own set of sport strategy and policy documents. Drawing on a sport for sport's sake approach (Collins, 2010), Sport Wales set out its vision: "to unite a sporting nation" through "every child hooked on sport" and "a nation of champions" (Sport Wales, 2011, p. 1). Accompanying this vision was a raft of other specific strategies (see Table 4.1) including the *Child Poverty Strategy* (Sport Wales, 2012a), the *Community Sport Strategy* (Sport Wales, 2012b), and the *Strategic Equality Plan* which has been updated (Sport Wales, 2013, 2016a). Taken together, these led to several significant programmes including Dragon Sport, 5 × 60, Free Swimming, Calls for Action, and the Healthy and Active Fund. Major strategic developments in performance sport included the *Coaching Strategy 2010–2016* (Sport Wales, 2010a), the *Governance and Leadership Framework for NGBs* (Sport Wales, 2015b, 2019), and the previously mentioned *Elite Sport Strategy* (Sport Wales, 2010b, 2015a).

The existence of two national strategies operating concurrently and largely in competition was highlighted in 2017 when stakeholders saw Sport Wales "at a crossroads in its strategic direction and the role it plays in the delivery of the well-being goals and government policy" (Welsh Government, 2017b, p. 3). The review which was invoked following internal difficulties made 20 recommendations. Welsh Government was asked to provide greater clarity around roles and responsibilities, and Sport Wales was required to change its ways of working and become more collaborative, transparent, and creative. One recommendation was the need for Sport Wales to develop a new, long-term strategy for sport which was positioned as being for the sector rather than for itself leading the sector. Following a national consultation, *Towards an Active Nation* was launched as the sector's long-term vision for sport in Wales (Sport Wales, 2018a) and was complemented by Sport Wales's own strategy (Sport Wales, 2018b).

Table 4.2 The Well-Being of Future Generations (Wales) Act 2015

The Seven Well-Being Goals	The Five Ways of Working
A prosperous Wales	Long-term
A resilient Wales	Integration
A healthier Wales	Involvement
A more equal Wales	Collaboration
A Wales of more cohesive communities	Prevention
A Wales of vibrant culture and thriving Welsh language	
A globally responsible Wales	

Two other national issues, enshrined in law, are important to Welsh sport policy since devolution. The first is the Welsh Language (Wales) Measure 2011 (National Assembly for Wales, 2011), which strengthens the equal status between English and Welsh and led recently to the Welsh Government setting a hugely ambitious target of one million Welsh speakers (about a third of the population) by 2050 (Welsh Government, 2017a). This has significant implications for public life in that the language will need to be spoken beyond the home and educational settings. Research by Evans et al. (2019) reveal that Welsh is not a living community sport language, and young Welsh people wishing to speak the heritage minority language may risk marginalisation because many local clubs are not ready to drive its promotion.

The second important feature of Welsh policy is the *Well-Being of Future Generations (Wales) Act 2015* (WBFGA) (Welsh Assembly Government, 2015). It establishes seven well-being goals and five ways of working (Table 4.2) and requires public accountability and greater collaboration from 44 public bodies. The WBFGA underpins the new vision for Sport in Wales (2018a) and Sport Wales's own strategy (2018b), and national indicator 38 is the percentage of people participating in sporting activities three or more times a week (Welsh Government 2021).

Elite sport

The development of elite sport in Wales has been cited as a policy strength (Welsh Government, 2017b), and as with other UK nations, the channelling of investment to those individuals and organisations who will make the greatest difference has become an important policy priority. Following the centralisation of UK Sport's World Class Programme, the *Elite Sport Strategy* (Sport Wales, 2010b, 2015a) focused on performance indicators which related to Commonwealth Games medals alongside the number of athletes representing Great Britain and Northern Ireland (GB&NI) in the Olympics and Paralympics. According to Sport Wales, "considering our size, Wales is a nation that very much punches above its weight in terms of sporting success: disability sport being a prime example" (Sport Wales, 2011, p. 15). The strategy affirmed its intent to work with those sports most likely to meet their targets and to emulate Australia and New Zealand – "nations world renowned for their commitment to sport and their drive for success" (p. 15).

Since devolution, there has been national success in football, with Wales reaching the semi-finals and quarter-finals of the Euros in 2016 and 2020 and playing in the FIFA World Cup Qatar 2022 for the first time since 1958. In rugby union, there has been Grand Slam and Six Nation success as well as World Cup quarter-finals in 1999, 2003, and 2015 and the semi-finals in 2011 and 2019. McInch and Fleming (2021, p. 8) conclude that the outcome of elite sport policy is that "Wales has experienced some impressive gains" and has been ambitious in its pursuit of excellence. In terms of medals, the 2018 Commonwealth Games was Team Wales's most successful haul with 36 medals (10 gold, 12 silver, and 14 bronze). The target was to be the number one nation (per capita) at the Commonwealth Games (Sport Wales, 2016b), but Wales came second to New Zealand on this measure. Targets for the Olympics were for Welsh athletes to account for 7% of GB&NI in Rio and 10% at subsequent games (Sport Wales, 2016b). In Rio 2016, 23/366 athletes representing GB&NI were Welsh, equating to 6% (McInch & Fleming, 2021). In Tokyo 2020 (+1), 26/376 athletes representing GB&NI were Welsh, equating to 6.9% winning 11 medals. There has also been consistent success by Disability Sport Wales and the performance of its athletes at major competitions. Interestingly, for the Commonwealth Games Birmingham 2022, no target was set (Sport Wales, 2022c).

Key to performance sport has been the development of national facilities and support given to athletes through using National Lottery funding. The performance-led sporting infrastructure is based on a blueprint for investment which includes two multi-sport national centres, the national pool in Swansea, the Geraint Thomas National Velodrome in Newport, and the National Indoor Athletics Centre in Cardiff. These are complemented by the re-development of other stadia, including the Principality and SWALEC stadia in Cardiff, the Ice Arena Wales, and the two principal football clubs of Swansea and Cardiff. It should be noted that Wales offers first-class natural facilities for outdoor sports across the country.

The Governance and Leadership Framework for Wales (GLFW) was initially developed in 2015 "by the sport sector, for the sport sector" and has subsequently been revised in 2019 to take account of national shifts in the landscape (Sport Wales, 2015b, 2019). Built around seven principles, it focuses on changing the culture of governance by emphasising board behaviours, which is also linked to a capability framework and public funding.

Founded in 1997, UK Sport aimed to create a successful elite sport system across the home nations; its 'no compromise' brand resulted in a target-driven, overarching framework which is punctuated for many sports every four years by the Commonwealth Games and annually by home championships. In Wales, success is measured, therefore, by both GB&NI selection and Commonwealth Games medals, which simultaneously and paradoxically requires home nations to offer a talent pipeline for athletes who have Olympic and World Championship podium potential as well as being nationally distinct to achieve Welsh victory. A further point of differentiation is that whilst Welsh elite sport policy has until recently (Sport Wales, 2022c) been results driven, UK Sport's 'no compromise' approach was not adopted. There remains a lack of independent research in this subject field, and thus, it is less clear whether elite sport in Wales has, as suggested by Green (2007) and Collins (2010), prospered at the expense of community and grassroots participation to which this chapter now turns.

Participation and community sport

Community sport is recognised to be complex and multifaceted (Coalter, 2007), and the Welsh landscape feels less coherent than some research indicates (McInch & Fleming, 2021), with evidence pointing to growing fragmentation and ambiguity. Three interconnected points provide important context. First, under devolution, there has been an explicit tension between sport and other agendas (especially health) and between the Welsh Government and Sport Wales (Welsh Government, 2017b). This has resulted in some policy gaps including, for example, broader physical activity, health, mental health, and community regeneration (Coalter, 2007) being overlooked. Whilst local authorities are involved in wide-ranging community initiatives, these have, until recently, been separate from Sport Wales's national sport policy. Second, the emphasis for over two decades on young people means that large cohorts of the population, including adults, the over 50s and families have been often overlooked. Whilst this could be explained by stretched resources and to a lesser extent confusion over national organisations' roles (specifically that of Sport Wales and Public Health Wales), it has impacted on the coherent development of community sport. Third, the level of socio-economic deprivation means that social justice has been a principal driver of the public policy agenda in Wales but one which sport has, until recently, remained immune to; in this regard, the policy emphasis has often been about developing sport in the community, rather than community sport development (Bolton et al., 2008a).

Participation rates sit at the heart of the community sport agenda, and given they have remained stubbornly low for over 20 years (National Assembly for Wales, 2014; Welsh Parliament, 2022), it is appropriately labelled a wicked issue. Men are more likely to participate than women, and adults from higher socio-economic groups are more likely to participate than those from lower socio-economic groups, ethnic minorities, or those living with a disability or in poverty. Recent evidence from 2019 to 2020[3] shows a pattern of participation with just under a third of adults (32% representing 808,000 people) meeting the Chief Medical Officer's target of participating in moderate intensity exercise three or more times a week, and worryingly, over a million adults (41%) had not participated in the previous four weeks (Sport Wales, 2020). For adults, the most popular activities are walking (2 miles or more), gym or fitness classes, swimming indoors, running and jogging outdoors, cycling, and outdoor football. Since 2020 and COVID-19, there have been impacts on sport and physical activity with data collection revealing many challenges, including a lack of opportunities to participate in organised sport and the need for a package of financial support for clubs and organisations throughout Wales (Sport Wales, 2021).

Aligned to the vision of every child hooked on sport, the *Community Sport Strategy 2012–20* (Sport Wales, 2012b) focused on five principal areas: thriving clubs, local decisions, quality education, committed workforce, and appropriate facilities. At its heart the community sport strategy was about getting more people involved and was reflected in the strapline, "from the 00s to the 000s" (Sport Wales, 2011, p. 5). Given the focus on clubs, coaches, and facilities, national governing bodies and local authorities were important agents for delivering the strategy. However, local authorities have seen sport and leisure as a lower priority than funding for education and social services, and the ongoing reduction in their budgets (Wales Audit Office, 2015) led the Independent Review to note the traditional sports development officer "has all but disappeared" (Welsh Government, 2017b, p. 14). Baker (2017) highlighted the challenges of fragmentation, collaborative dissonance, and future roles which alongside other evidence led to a recommendation for regionalisation and the creation of five Regional Sport Partnerships, with North Wales being the most advanced. These Regional Sport Partnerships will replace the separate funding of 22 unitary councils.

In terms of public interventions at the community level, there have been some significant programmes targeting young people linked to extracurricular sport which are considered in the next section. Wales's Free Swimming initiative is Europe's longest running public community, leisure and health intervention. Commencing as a pilot in 2003, it was quickly rolled out by all 22 local authorities to target young people aged 16 and under and those aged 60+. The initiative had multiple objectives and iterations (for a full discussion, see Bolton & Martin, 2013; Anderson et al., 2014), which led to changes that reflected different priorities, including, for example, structured swims over free splash and learn to swim programmes over holiday fun. Similar to other welfare initiatives including free prescriptions and free breakfasts for school children (Andrews & Martin, 2010), it retained its central premise of being free at the point of delivery. At an initial annual cost of £2.4 million (increasing to £3.5 million), it is the single most significant public leisure intervention in Wales, and its early impact (Bolton et al., 2008b) led in 2008 to the launch of a national free swimming programme in England albeit culled in 2010 as part of the UK Government's austerity measures. Following a second independent review (UKRCS, 2018) in which free swimming was no longer seen as fit for purpose, revised schemes targeting young people from deprived areas as well as introducing a broader offer for older people (which includes dryside and wetside activities) was introduced.

Physical education and school sport

The importance attached to young people by Sport Wales (Sports Council for Wales, 1997; Sport Wales, 2011) is arguably the policy centrepiece, in which the links between physical education (PE), school sport, and community are brought together. In this domain, by putting young people first, Welsh sport policy has looked to be far more interconnected. Through the adoption of physical activity guidelines, the policy framework has been shaped externally by the UK Chief Medical Officers and the World Health Organisation which led Sport Wales to establish a requirement of five hours of moderate to vigorous intensity exercise a week, being divided between curriculum and non-curriculum time.

Young people's participation in sport and physical activity is, therefore, one important measure, and recent research (Richards et al., 2022) has revealed significant ongoing challenges if targets are to be met. Sport Wales itself has undertaken five separate surveys from 2011 to 2022[4] in which longitudinal analysis suggests participation falls short of the CMO recommendations and Sport Wales's previous impact measure of "75% of children and young people hooked on sport in 2026" (Sport Wales, 2016, p. 16). Whilst the results from 2018 revealed that participation had been sustained since the previous one in 2015 with 48% of young people taking part in organised sport three or more times a week (in addition to curriculum lessons), the most recent survey shows a 9% decrease, with only 39% meeting the target (Sport Wales, 2022d). This decline points to the significant impact the pandemic has had on young people and their participation which is further exacerbated by other demographic characteristics. For example, the 2018 survey showed increased participation among females (46%, up from 44% in 2015), but in 2022, this figure had regressed to 36% and a similar picture emerges when looking at ethnicity and disability. Most notable has been the widening participation gap from 13% in 2018 to 15% in 2022 of those living in socio-economic deprivation (Sport Wales, 2022d).

With 36% of young people reporting no frequent participation outside of the curriculum (Sport Wales, 2022d), it is striking that Green et al.'s observation (2005, p. 30) nearly 20 years ago remains relevant, "… just as with adults, there is a significant minority of young people doing relatively little or absolutely nothing". Given the intractable nature of this issue, different policy responses are needed, and academics have an important role in developing innovative research that might present new theoretical understandings and conceptual frameworks.

Policy development embraces the three settings of PE, school sport (linked largely in Wales to extracurricular sport) and community sport. Figure 4.1 (UKRCS, 2019) provides a timeline of policy, programmes, and initiatives undertaken between 2000 and 2018. With regard to mainstream PE, the report identified key contributions in relation to curriculum resources, workforce skills, quality standards through the PE and School Sport (PESS) programme plus later the Physical Literacy Programme for Schools (PLPS), and the highly successful Young Ambassadors' programme. In terms of extracurricular opportunities, the Active Young People Programmes (AYPP) were managed by each local authority and focused on increasing young people's participation, predominantly in school settings via two

72 Nicola Bolton

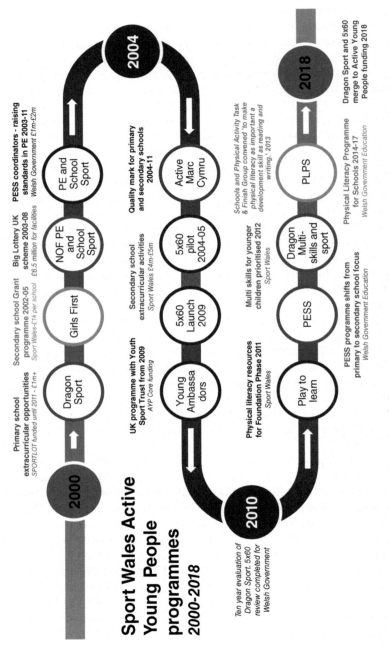

Figure 4.1 Sport Wales's Active Young People Programmes.
Source: UKRCS (2019).

flagship programmes: Dragon Multi-Skills and Sport(primary schools) and 5 × 60 (secondary schools). Costing approximately £1 million and £4 million, respectively, the conclusion of the review suggested that whilst Sport Wales had worked well with schools and leisure departments, the impact on mainstream education departments was limited (UKRCS, 2019).

Two examples demonstrate the challenges encountered in shaping PE policy in relation to young people's physical literacy and activity. First, a Welsh Government commissioned review was led by Dame Tanni Grey-Thompson with the remit of how to develop the role of schools in increasing levels of physical activity. Its single recommendation was that "Physical Education becomes a core subject of the national curriculum in Wales" (Welsh Government, 2013, p. 16) and whilst supported by the National Assembly for Wales (2014, para. 111–112) it was not implemented. The second, and linked challenge to school-based PE in Wales is that under the reforms to the new curriculum (Welsh Government, 2020) PE will be placed under the Health and Wellbeing Area of Learning and Experience. This is a policy shift which brings challenges both for the future training of PE in Wales and the likelihood of greater dissonance between the UK home nations.

Funded by the Welsh Government and National Lottery, Sport Wales's two flagship programmes of Dragon Sport (for primary aged school children) and 5 × 60 (for secondary school children) operated for nearly two decades. Both extracurricular physical activity programmes sat separate from the curriculum (and PE departments), and had the twin aims, to offer sporting opportunities to young people and develop links between schools and communities. Whilst Dragon Sport focused more on physical literacy, the 5 × 60 scheme aimed to engage less active pupils through an 'opt in, opt out' philosophy (Bolton et al., 2007). In terms of 5 × 60, research revealed that young people "relished the element of choice and ownership provided by the different and exciting activities like street dance, fencing, gorge walking, surfing, roller hockey, dodgeball, cheerleading and climbing" (Bryant et al., 2016, p. 50). Resources proved difficult to sustain for both programmes, and there were challenges relating to the supply of local coaches and links to community clubs. In many cases, schools were overly reliant on the 5 × 60 officers providing after-school activities. Research on the implications of 5 × 60 programme sitting separate from a school's PE department has revealed both strengths (Bryant et al., 2016) and limitations (Rainer et al., 2015). In this regard, it is worth noting that were significant differences between extracurricular sport policy development in Wales compared to England and Scotland

(Rainer et al., 2015). The new strategic framework (Sport Wales, 2018a, 2018b) introduced some significant changes with active young people remaining a priority for Sport Wales but as part of a wider policy agenda.

Sport development programmes and policies

It is widely acknowledged that sport development is a contested concept in the UK, and as devolution has gathered momentum, this has been evident in Wales. Against a backdrop of stretched resources, Sport Wales has been an advocate for, and at times protector of, a sport for sport's sake approach over a more pluralistic agenda that promotes the wider benefits of sport (Coalter, 2007; Collins, 2010). Important to Sport Wales has been the significance of retaining a whole systems approach for sport (Collins et al., 2012), which encompasses the three worlds of participation, performance sport and elite. The delivery of sport policy has shown an emphasis on young people with an ambition that every child will be "hooked on sport" (Sport Wales, 2011, p. 4). This has been addressed by focusing on physical literacy and a raft of curricular and extracurricular programmes alongside important community sport initiatives which have focused on coaches and volunteers.

In contrast, the promotion of physical activity and its wider benefits (Coalter, 2007) has, with the exception of free swimming, been more ad hoc. It is worth noting that as a Welsh Government-led initiative, free swimming, struggled with multiple objectives and implementation issues, even though its overarching aim was to increase physical activity (not necessarily sports participation) and to ensure it was universally available and free at the point of delivery (Bolton & Martin, 2013). Thus, the wider benefits of sport and physical activity (Coalter, 2007) have become more prominent in policy debates as devolution became firmly established and the influence of the WBFGA becomes more embedded.

The Calls for Action initiative provides further evidence of sport fulfilling a broader agenda. Initially introduced in 2012, it operated over two separate phases (2012–2015 and 2014–2018) with a rationale to promote community sport (Sport Wales, 2012a, 2012b) and create a legacy from London 2012. However, the focus changed significantly from phase 1 which sought to invest in facilities to an agenda in phase 2 that explicitly aimed to tackle inequalities (Bolton et al., 2018) and seek engagement with hard-to-reach groups. This was broadly successful although research (Dashper et al., 2019) revealed a significant gap in terms of working within black, Asian, and minority ethnic (BAME) communities. Overall, the programme was commended for its innovative and learning approach (Welsh Government, 2017b), and building on this success, a £5.4 million programme called the Healthy and Active Fund (HAF) was launched to address physical activity. Informed by the WBFGA, this initiative forms part of a formal cross-sector collaboration (Kolovou et al., 2022) between Welsh Government, Sport Wales, Public Health Wales, and Natural Resources Wales.

The WBFGA also informed the new vision for sport in Wales (Sport Wales, 2018a) and Sport Wales's own strategy (2018b). The launch of this vision and strategy reflects a transformative change in the organisation of sport and physical activity in Wales. It has been spearheaded by Sport Wales which has moved from grant funder to that of agent, adviser, advocate, and facilitator. The explicit shift to an insight-led approach which uses theory of change (Bolton et al., 2018) has also benefited from specialist independent advice given by two advisory groups comprising representatives from the eight Welsh HEIs that focus on (1) performance and elite sport and (2) physical activity and well-being. The WBFGA ensures the emphasis on health and well-being remains a dominant driver for community sport participation as evidenced by the national strategy, *Healthy Weight: Health Wales* (Welsh Government, 2019).

It is anticipated that the establishment of the Regional Sport Partnerships (which are underway) will take the lead in managing much of this work in that they will be responsible for the development and resource allocation of community sport. Thus, there are likely to be challenges, perhaps risks, for local organisations which will be expected to find increasingly innovative and partnership-based solutions to local and regional problems. Furthermore, whilst there are some likely managerial and efficiency advantages in moving from 22 local authorities to five regional partnerships, the effectiveness of these changes is, as yet, unproven and may not be sufficient to address the sport policy challenges outlined in this chapter.

Challenges and barriers to facilitating sport development

Wales has a diverse sporting landscape which has changed significantly since the establishment of the Sports Council for Wales in 1972 and the creation of the Welsh Assembly in 1999. This penultimate section discusses four strategic challenges associated with the changing sport policy landscape in Wales.

The first challenge is whether Welsh sport policy should be distinct from that of other home nations. Mackintosh (2021) notes that given the size of England, most research is written from an Anglo-centric perspective, and thus, academics have assumed their research 'speaks' for the smaller UK nations. The creation of Sports Wales as an independent organisation over five decades ago reflected the distinct character of Wales, its people, and its sporting history.

Under devolution, policy development has become far more wide-ranging, and this has ensured that sport policy at both elite and community levels has become more, not less, distinct from the other UK home nations, especially England. The role of politics and policy development in the Welsh Government is highly instructive. Labour's dominance has provided some degree of policy continuity in Wales but has also ensured 'clear red water' (Drakeford, 2006) between Welsh and English policy agendas – for example, the WBFGA and the new national curriculum. Thus, while many challenges are shared across the home nations, the policy options and responses will differ and will, in turn, require academic researchers to become aware of policy distinctiveness in each of the home nations (Mackintosh, 2021).

A second challenge which is shared by all home nations is the intractable and thus wicked issue of participation in sport and physical activity or, more to the point, non-participation. Whilst physical inactivity is a UK-wide issue among the population at large, this chapter has shown that evidence points to specific barriers experienced among 'hard-to-reach' communities and that these are often linked to health. In terms of 'hard-to-reach' populations in Wales, the lower levels of participation found among women and individuals living with a disability, from a BAME background and/or living in poverty, are now the focus of policymakers and practitioners. The role of academics in exploring new approaches in which social innovation and local solutions can be evidenced could be important and contrasts with traditional top-down government-led sport policy strategies.

Financial resources is a third shared challenge and cuts across the sporting landscape in terms of people, places, and infrastructure. Whilst Lindsey and Houlihan (2013) suggest increased Welsh Government spending under devolution, the decline in expenditure by local authorities suggests retrenchment (Wales Audit Office, 2015). As a non-statutory service, there are insufficient resources for the effective and sustained implementation of sport policy, which has resulted in years of flip-flopping (Collins, 2010) between participation and performance. Furthermore, the lack of clarity to articulate the contribution that sport makes to the public policy agenda (Coalter, 2007) has led to the pursuit of multiple objectives and fuzzy implementation

(Bolton & Martin, 2013). Whilst England pursued a target-driven culture, a more collaborative but arguably less effective approach was adopted in Wales (Andrews & Martin, 2010). The overall squeeze on public finances has led local authorities to pass over management of community assets to local community groups and, in some cases, has even led to the closure of community sport and recreation facilities.

The fourth and final challenge is linked to the need for ongoing development of research and evidence. The past two decades have seen a growth in the evidence base to support sport policy, and whilst the production of this text is reflective of this growth, there remain ongoing challenges. In Wales, sport policy research has attracted growing interest but remains relatively underdeveloped. Areas of policy research which might be of interest are the consideration of cross-sector partnerships, governance, innovation, community asset transfers, whole systems approaches, and sustainable changes in participation. There remains also a need for the exploration of new methods and approaches which can support and underpin evidence-based policy.

Summary

This chapter has considered the development of sport policy in Wales and revealed a complex and changing landscape. Whilst there are connections to the other home nations, especially England, the independence of Sports Wales means sport policy has never been a branch of Sport England. Devolution has created more distinctiveness. The development of Welsh sport policy over the past 20 years is inextricably linked to the Welsh Government – policy and politics are entwined. The Welsh Language, the WBFGA, and changes to health, education, and the economy all point to a growing and distinct policy agenda in which sport will need to articulate its relevance. Whilst short-term policy is likely to be structured around the three pillars of elite, community, and schools, this might change. The WBFGA might create an environment in which sport genuinely straddles different policy domains – with elite sport and sport development attached to the economy; physical activity attached to health and well-being; and young people and school sport attached to education but with an emphasis on health and well-being. The future role of elite sport could also be significant should the Welsh Government pursue its major events strategy with a renewed confidence and desire to build Welsh identity by hosting a multi-sport event, such as the Commonwealth Games.

Acknowledgement

The author is extremely grateful to Steve Martin who is Director of the Wales Centre for Public Policy and Professor of Public Policy and Management at Cardiff University for his insightful feedback on an earlier draft.

Notes

1 Sport Wales is its trade name and for consistency purposes this will be used for in-text citation within the chapter.
2 The evolution of devolution in Wales has led to various changes to the National Assembly for Wales – for consistency purposes in-text citation will hereafter refer to Welsh Government and Senedd Cymru.
3 Data on sport and active lifestyles forms part of the Welsh Government's National Survey for Wales which involves annually face-to-face interviews with over 12,000 randomly selected individuals.
4 Surveys undertaken in 2011, 2013, 2015, 2018 and 2022 (which included over 116,000 children from 1,000 schools).

References

Anderson, M., Bolton, N., Davies, B. & Fleming, S. (2014). Local implementation of national policy: A case-study critique of the free swimming initiative for the 60 plus population. *Managing Leisure*, 19(2), 151–165. doi:10.10 80/13606719.2013.859456.
Andrews, R. & Martin, S. J. (2010). Regional variations in public service outcomes: The impact of policy divergence in England, Scotland and Wales. *Regional Studies*, 44, 919–934.
Baker, C. (2017). *Coordination of community sport development in Wales: An investigation of stakeholder perspectives concerning the organisation and structure of community sport in Wales.* University of Gloucester.
Bolton, N., Fleming, S. & Elias, B. (2008a). The experience of community sport development: A case study of Blaenau Gwent. *Managing Leisure*, 13, 92–103.
Bolton, N., Fleming, S. & Galdes, M. (2007). Physical activity programmes in secondary schools in Wales: Implications from a pilot scheme. *Managing Leisure*, 12, 74–88. doi:10.1080/13606710601071579.
Bolton, N. & Martin, S. (2013). The policy and politics of free swimming. *International Journal of Sport Policy and Politics*, 5(3), 445–463. doi:10.1080 /19406940.2012.656689.
Bolton, N., Martin, S., Anderson, M., Smith, B. & Jennings. C. (2008b). *Free swimming: An evaluation of the National Assembly Government's initiative.* Sports Council for Wales.
Bolton, N., Martin, S., Grace, C. & Harris, S. (2018). Implementing a theory of change approach to research sport participation programmes targeting

'hard to reach' groups. *International Journal of Sport Policy and Politics. Special Issue: Theory and Methods in Sport Policy and Politics*, 10, 761–777. doi:10.1080/19406940.2018.1476397.

Bryant, A., Bolton, N. & Fleming, S. (2016). Extracurricular sport and physical activity in Welsh secondary schools: Leisure lifestyles and young people. *Journal of Physical Education and Sports Management*, 2(2), 41–55. doi:10.15640/jpesm.v2n2a4.

Coalter, F. (2007). *A wider role for sport: Who's keeping the score*. Routledge.

Collins, D., Bailey, R., Ford, P. A., MacNamara, A., Toms, M. & Pearce, G. (2012). Three worlds: New directions in participant development in sport and physical activity. *Sport, Education and Society*, 17(2), 225–243.

Collins, M. (2010). From 'sport for good' to 'sport for sport's sake' – Not a good move for sports development in England? *International Journal of Sport Policy*, 2(3), 367–379.

Dashper, K., Fletcher, T. & Long, J. (2019). 'Intelligent investment'? Welsh sport policy and the (in)visibility of 'race'. *Leisure Studies*, 38(6), 762–774.

Davies, L. & Kokolakakis, T. (2018). *Measuring the social and economic value of sport in Wales*. Report 2: The economic importance of sport in Wales 2016/17. Sport Industry Research Centre, Sheffield Hallam University and Sport Wales.

Drakeford, M. (2006). Healthy policy in Wales: Making a difference in conditions of difficulty. *Critical Social Policy*, 26, 543–561.

Evans, L., Bolton, N., Jones, C. & Iorwerth, H. (2019). 'Defnyddiwch y Gymraeg'!: Community sport as a vehicle for encouraging the use of the Welsh language. *Sport in Society: Community Sport and Social Inclusion: International Perspectives*, 22(6), 1115–1129.

Green, K., Smith, A. & Roberts, K. (2005). Young people and lifelong participation in sport and physical activity: A sociological perspective on contemporary physical education programmes in England and Wales. *Leisure Studies*, 24, 27–42.

Green, M. (2007). Olympic glory or grassroots development? Sports policy priorities in Australia, Canada and the United Kingdom 1960–2006. *International Journal of the History of Sport*, 24, 921–953.

Houlihan, B. & White, A. (2002). *The politics of sport development*. Routledge.

Kolovou, V., Bolton, N. & Crone, D. (2022). A systematic review and qualitative meta-synthesis of the context, barriers and facilitators to cross-sector collaboration promoting physical activity (PO2–03). *European Journal of Public Health*, 32, 2. doi:10.1093/eurpub/ckac095.022.

Lindsey, I. & Houlihan, B. (2013). *Sport policy in Britain*. Routledge.

Mackintosh, C. (2021). *Foundations of sport development*. Taylor and Francis Group.

McInch, A. & Fleming, S. (2021). Sport policy formation and enactment in post-devolution Wales: 1999–2020. *International Journal of Sport Policy and Politics*. doi:10.1080/19406940.2021.1996438.

Morgan, K. & Upton, S. (2005). *Culling the quangos: The new governance and public service reform in Wales*. School of City and Regional Planning, Cardiff University.

Murphy, L. J., Pickernell, D., Thomas, B. & Fuller, D. (2017). Innovation, social capital and regional policy: The case of the communities first programme in Wales. *Regional Studies, Regional Science*, 5(1), 21–39.

National Assembly for Wales (2011). *Welsh language (Wales) measure 2011*. National Assembly for Wales.

National Assembly for Wales (2014). *Participation levels in sport. Report of the Communities, Equality and Local Government Committee.* National Assembly for Wales.

Office for National Statistics (2022). *Population and household estimates, Wales: Census 2021*. https://www.ons.gov.uk/peoplepopulationandcommun ity/populationandmigration/populationestimates/bulletins/population andhouseholdestimateswales/census2021.

Rainer, P., Griffiths, R., Cropley, B. & Jarvis, S. (2015). Barriers to delivering extracurricular school sport and physical activity in Wales: a qualitative study of 5x60 officers' views and perspectives. *Journal of Physical Activity and Health*, 12(2), 245–252. doi:10.1123/jpah.2012-0476.

Richards, A. B., Mackintosh, K. A., Swindell, N., Ward, M., Marchant, E., James, M., Edwards, L. C., Tyler, R., Blain, D., Wainwright, N., Nicholls, S., Mannello, M., Morgan, K., Evans, T. & Stratton, G. (2022). WALES 2021 active healthy kids (AHK) report card: The fourth pandemic of childhood inactivity. *International Journal of Environmental Research and Public Health*, 19, 8138. doi:10.3390/ijerph19138138.

Robinson, L. (2004). *Managing public sport and leisure services*. Routledge.

Sports Council for Wales (1986). *Changing needs: Changing times*. Sport Wales.

Sports Council for Wales (1989). *Changing needs: Changing times, a strategy review*. Sport Wales.

Sports Council for Wales (1997). *Putting young people first*. Sport Wales.

Sports Wales (2010a). *Coaching strategy 2010–2016*. Sport Wales.

Sport Wales (2010b). *Elite sport strategy 2010–2016*. Sport Wales.

Sport Wales (2011). *A vision for sport in Wales*. Sport Wales.

Sport Wales (2012a). *Child poverty strategy*. Sport Wales.

Sport Wales (2012b). *Community sport strategy 2012–20*. Sport Wales.

Sport Wales (2013). *Strategic equality plan 2012–2016*. Sport Wales.

Sport Wales (2015a). *Elite sport strategy*. Sport Wales.

Sport Wales (2015b). *Governance and leadership framework in Wales*. Sport Wales.

Sport Wales (2016a). *Strategic equality plan 2016–2020*. Sport Wales.

Sport Wales (2016b). *This is Sport Wales: Business plan 2016–17*. Sport Wales.

Sport Wales (2018a). *A vision for sport*. Sport Wales.

Sport Wales (2018b). *Enabling sport in Wales to thrive: Our ambition and purpose*. Sport Wales.

Sport Wales (2019). *Governance and leadership framework in Wales*. Sport Wales.

Sport Wales (2020). *National survey for Wales 2019–20: Sport and active lifestyles*. Sport Wales.

Sport Wales (2021). *Sport Wales annual report 2020–21.* Sport Wales.
Sport Wales (2022a, October 19). *Royal charter.* https://www.sport.wales/content-vault/key-publications/#:~:text=Sport%20Wales%20was%20established%20by,the%20provision%20of%20facilities%20thereto.
Sport Wales (2022b, October 19). *Sporting activities and governing bodies recognised by the Sports Councils.* Retrieved from http://www.sport.wales/content-vault/recognition-of-sports-and-national-governing-bodies/.
Sport Wales (2022c, November 20). *Medal target?... "We haven't got one".* Retrieved from https://www.sport.wales/media-centre/latest-news/medal-targetwe-havent-got-one/.
Sport Wales (2022d, November 19). *School sport survey.* Retrieved from https://www.sport.wales/research-and-insight/school-sport-survey/.
Tewdwr-Jones, M. (2001). Planning and the National Assembly for Wales: Generating distinctiveness and inclusiveness in a new political context. *European Planning Studies,* 9, 553–562.
Torrance, D. (2022). *Devolution in Wales: "A process, not an event".* Commons library briefing, 4th May 2022. Number CBP8318. House of Commons Library.
UKRCS (2018). *Free swimming in Wales: A review.* An independent report prepared for Sport Wales. https://democracy.npt.gov.uk/documents/s52972/Free%20Swimming%20Report%20Final.pdf [Accessed 22 August 2022].
UKRCS (2019). *Sport Wales' young people programmes review.* Final report prepared for Sport Wales by UKRCS.
Wales Audit Office (2015). *Delivering with less – Leisure services.* Wales Audit Office.
Welsh Assembly Government (2005). *Climbing higher – The Welsh Assembly Government strategy for sport and physical activity.* Welsh Assembly Government.
Welsh Assembly Government (2006). *Climbing higher: Next steps.* Welsh Assembly Government.
Welsh Assembly Government (2009). *Creating an active Wales.* Welsh Assembly Wales.
Welsh Assembly Government (2010). *Event Wales: A major events strategy for Wales 2010–2020.* Welsh Assembly Government.
Welsh Assembly Government (2013). *Physical literacy – An all-Wales approach to increasing levels of physical activity for children and young people. Schools and physical activity task and finish group.* Welsh Government.
Welsh Assembly Government (2015). *Well-being of future generations (Wales) act.* Welsh Government.
Welsh Government (2016). *Summary of Wales 2026 Commonwealth Games feasibility study.* Welsh Government.
Welsh Government (2017a). *Cymraeg 2050: A million Welsh speakers.* Welsh Government.
Welsh Government (2017b). *Sport Wales review, an independent report.* Welsh Government.

Welsh Government (2019). *Healthy weight: Health Wales.* Welsh Government.
Welsh Government (2020). *Introduction to curriculum for Wales guidance [online].* Welsh Government. Retrieved from https://hwb.gov.wales/curriculum-for-wales/introduction/.
Welsh Government (2021). *Well-being of future generations: National indicators and national milestones for Wales.* Retrieved from https://gov.wales/sites/default/files/publications/2021-12/national-indicators-and-milestones-for-wales-2021.pdf.
Welsh Government (2022). *The national events strategy: 2022–2030.* Welsh Government.
Welsh Parliament (2022). *Levelling the playing field: A report on the participation in sport and physical activity in disadvantages areas.* Welsh Parliament.

5 Sport Policy in Northern Ireland

Kyle Ferguson, Paul Donnelly, Robert Heyburn, and Simon Shibli

Overview and structure of sport

Northern Ireland (NI) is the smallest of the home nations – which constitute the United Kingdom – in terms of both geography (13,843 km, 6%) and population (1.8 m, 2.8%) (Breuer et al., 2015). The economy of NI is heavily dependent on the public sector for employment, with some of the highest levels of unemployment in the UK. Since the signing of the Belfast Agreement in 1998, Northern Ireland has been emerging from a 30-year conflict (colloquially known as the "Troubles") into a vibrant service sector led economy with considerable tourism (and in particular sports tourism) and inward investment.

As mentioned in the introductory chapter, the structure of sport in the UK is complex. A simplistic representation as far as NI is concerned (Sport NI, 2012, 2018) is provided in Figure 5.1. For example, although NI is part of the UK, its athletes have the choice of competing for the UK or the Republic of Ireland. NI competes in international competition in its own right, in sports such as Association Football and Netball as well as in the Commonwealth Games which is managed by the NI Commonwealth Games Council. Furthermore, some sports such as rugby union and boxing are organised on an all-Ireland basis, with branches operating at a provincial level (e.g., Ulster Rugby and Ulster Boxing Council). NI is the only home nation that has specific legislation, namely the *Belfast Agreement 1998*, which aims to ensure that due consideration is given to equality of opportunity and good relations when governing, promoting, and delivering sport as noted in the 'parity of esteem' concept. The complex geopolitics of NI and its relationships with the rest of the United Kingdom (UK) and the Republic of Ireland (ROI) require NI to have strategic partnerships and pathways in place with both countries to enable its athletes and competitors to reach their full potential.

DOI: 10.4324/9781003241232-5

Sport Northern Ireland (SNI) is charged by the Department for Communities (DfC) with the development and delivery of sport in the region and enjoys the status of being a National Lottery fund distributor. SNI is tasked with developing and enhancing the sporting sector in NI, including financial investment in governing bodies, district councils, sports clubs, and athletes. Operating across its three sites consisting of its headquarters in Belfast, the elite Sport NI Sports Institute (SNISI) in Jordanstown, and the outdoor adventure centre at Tollymore, SNI works closely with UK Sport, Sport Ireland, and the relevant Olympic and Paralympic councils, while locally the NI Sports Forum represents the governing bodies of sport across NI. Figure 5.1 provides a representation of the relationships between the various UK

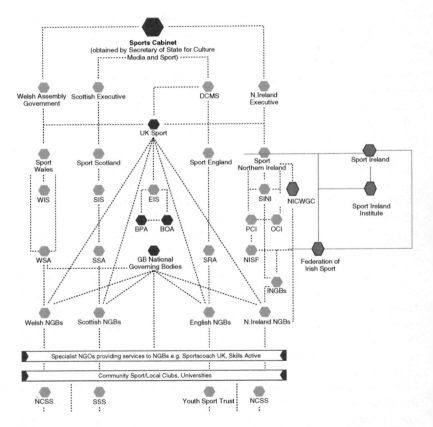

Figure 5.1 The structure of sport in the United Kingdom and Republic of Ireland.

and ROI sports bodies, which illustrate the complexities of the sporting landscape within which NI is located. Aspects from this structure will be discussed further across this chapter.

Brief evolution of sport policy and politics

The evolution of sport policy in NI has been greatly influenced by both the political and social realities which have shaped the complex public sector and sporting structures in NI. The significance was summarised by Houlihan (1997) who noted that to understand why governments act in a particular manner we must consider the cultural, ideological, and historical context. This section takes cognisance of the importance of context (Ferguson et al., 2017; Sugden, 2010; Coalter, 2009) by reflecting on the recent modernisation agenda across the public sector in NI (Birrell, 2014; Bairner, 2013), fuelled by a prolonged period of austerity and government inactivity by reviewing the social circumstances and conditions in which sporting programmes operate in NI.

The key historic developments impacting sport policy and politics in Northern Ireland can be summarised as follows:

- Partition
- Period of Troubles
- Post conflict structures (Belfast Agreement)
- Reform of public administration and the transition from output-driven policy to an outcomes-based approach.
- Creation of National Lottery and recognition of sport as a good cause
- Dual nationality and sporting governance structures
- Establishment of National Institute for Sports

The partition of Ireland in 1921 separated Ireland into two self-governing entities namely, Northern Ireland and the Republic of Ireland. Prior to partition, many sporting bodies of the day were organised on an all-Ireland basis with all Ireland teams. Subsequently, individual governing bodies of sport determined differing structures governed by either a national governing body representative of six counties of NI, nine counties of provincial Ulster, 32 country All Ireland or four nations of the UK, adding complication to sport policy in NI. Nevertheless, Sport NI only recognises – and thus invests in – one governing body for each sport in NI as defined within the UK Sports Council's Recognition Policy in 2017.

During a sustained period of violence (1960s–1998) commonly referred to as the "Troubles", the European Union designated NI as economically disadvantaged and socially deprived. Society faced widespread segregation in all aspects of life from education to housing resulting in the formation of single entity communities (Bush & Houston, 2012). Segregation extended to sports, with sports associated with one side of the community or the other with only limited examples of cross-community participation (boxing and football). Sporting emblems, venues, and sporting colours were perceived as politicoreligious markers (Mitchell et al., 2016). This led the UK government to invest in leisure provision across Belfast in the 1970s, by providing shared leisure spaces and using sport to break down barriers; however, the desired impact was short-lived, leading Huntley (1988) to suggest that promoting a sporting solution to a political problem was unrealistic.

Control and responsibility for the governing of NI alternated between direct rule (1972–1999 and 2002 until 2007) from London and various devolved agreements (1999–2002 and 2007–2016) (Elliot et al., 2012). The signing of the Belfast Agreement in 1998 brought relative peace to NI and with this multi-layers of governance across the political environment (Birrell, 2014) with varying degrees of influence from the EU, the UK, and the Republic of Ireland. Although the ambitious agreement brought about peace and joint governance, some commentators have criticised the Agreement for leaving unresolved legacy issues described as the institutionalisation of sectarian differences as opposed to their eradication (Bairner, 2013).

Northern Ireland remains reliant on UK public sector funding to deliver public services (Haase, 2018). In this context, sport has benefited from public sector funding across the years, based on what government saw as the potential social benefits of sport. Nonetheless, the reliance on funding – like other areas of the UK – changed the focus beyond traditional sports development (Houlihan & White, 2002). The so-called 'Peace Dividend' saw funding released to support the third sector in building community relations under a policy ethos of 'parity of esteem' whereby both communities 'Protestant and Catholic' should be treated equally. Sport was identified as one vehicle to support this work through engaging with underrepresented groups, promoting cross-community engagement and encouraging participation in sport. At an elite level, the Belfast Agreement (1998) enshrined the rights of athletes in NI to compete for Ireland, GB or NI in international competition, dependant on the pathway offered by the governing bodies. This has brought many unique challenges to those bodies responsible for governing, promoting, and delivering sport – a result of the unresolved identity issues within the Belfast Agreement previously noted by Bairner (2013) – which have a direct impact on recognition, representation, flags, and anthems.

Since the signing of the Belfast Agreement, a growing emphasis has been placed on the role of what are referred to as 'grassroots' delivery agents (including sports) from the voluntary and community (third) sector to assist government in achieving their objectives as part of a local collaborative approach (Bush & Houston, 2012). The economic focus presented within the Programme for Government (2011–2015) promoted global growth and inward direct investment as key outcomes. Each government department retained responsibility for their targeted areas with vastly contrasting aims and objectives. Under these circumstances, sport continued to be adopted as part of a one-size-fits-all toolkit for tackling vastly contrasting social, economic, and health issues by each government department.

The reform of public services in NI (2008) saw 12 departments reduced to 9. Specifically, this had a major impact on sport. Formerly under the control of the Department of Culture, Arts and Leisure, the reform saw responsibility for sport move to the newly formed Department for Communities (DfC). In financial terms, moving from a relatively small department representing approximately 1% (£89.9 million) of the 2015–2016 NI Executive Budget (NI Executive Budget 2015–2016) to the new larger department representing approximately 8.5% (£872 million) of the NI Executive Budget (NI Executive Budget 2017–2018). The importance of this change relates to the challenge of accessing funding within a larger department with a wider range of competing priorities and maintaining the profile of sport to achieve this.

The Department for Communities (DfC) is responsible for the central strategic administration and promotion of sport in NI and the sponsorship of its arm's length body – Sport NI, which was established as the lead delivery agency for sport in NI. DfC itself has responsibility for a diverse portfolio of social policies, each competing for funding – as modernisation cuts continue to be implemented – while at the same time tasked with working collaboratively to achieve mutual goals.

The Programme for Government (PfG) sets the strategic direction for all policy activities in NI. Alignment of sport policy is then agreed in the form of the ten-year departmental strategy. This strategy is then operationalised with its high-level aims linked to the objectives laid out in the SNI Corporate Plan (normally covering a five-year period) and annual business plans.

The 2016 Draft PfG transitioned to an evidence-based outcomes-driven approach to policy known as outcomes-based accountability (Friedman, 2005), consisting of a two-tier model of outcomes and indicators employed to assess both organisational performance and population impact. The process maximises the contribution of all partners and stakeholders by creating shared ownership. Initially constructed around a framework of 14 strategic outcomes, the objective was to promote collaborative and co-design approaches between public, private, and third sectors to work across boundaries while focusing on outcomes rather than departmental outputs. The performance accountability then distinguishes between quality and quantity using three measures: How much did we do? How well did we do it? And is anyone better off?

Caution has been raised in relation to the potential impact on sporting organisations, as this type of policy transition (outputs to outcomes) may increase pressure for sporting programmes to straddle institutional boundaries, while still providing evidence of both programme development and programme outcome (Adams & Harris, 2014). Consequently, influence is placed on sports organisations to compromise objectives to secure funding rather than contributing to the development of a clearly defined sustainable sports sector.

Contextually, in sport the potential garnered from the introduction of the outcomes-based framework has been hampered until very recently by the absence of a relevant government indicator within the programme for government. The most recent draft (2021) for public consultation includes – for the first time – a specific government indicator related to 'Physical Health and Well-Being', requiring all departments to evidence their contribution to sport and physical activity.

Sport NI funding emanates from two main sources: exchequer funding direct from DfC (NI Block Grant) and National Lottery funding from the Department for Digital, Culture, Media and Sport providing an annual budget of approximately £27 million (Sport NI Business Plan 2021–2022) to deliver two sporting outcomes: (1) *People in Northern Ireland adopting and sustaining participation in sport and physical activity*, and (2) *NI athletes among the best in the world*. Outcome 1 sits comfortably within the PfG contributing to eight indicators compared to outcome 2 which contributes to one government indicator (Sport NI, 2021). The two outcomes are reflective of traditional sports development – focusing on participation and performance – which creates a potential void in relation to sport for development. The Executive Office administrates specific cross-community sport-related funding schemes under the *Together: Building a United Community (T:BUC) Strategy 2013*.

The Local Government Act (NI) 2014 also placed a duty on local authorities to initiate, facilitate, and maintain community planning in their respective areas through localised collaborative approaches inclusive of sport. Promoting the role of sport in collaborative discussions with a range of statutory partners established 11 community plans within the Local Government (Community Planning Partners) Order (NI) 2016. While creating enhanced community programming at a local council level, this approach established 11 separate community plans with implications for those working across NI as a whole.

The *Active Living – Sport and Physical Activity Strategy* (2022) expands the reach of sport and addresses the absence of a national physical activity strategy in NI. In so doing, the *Active Living Strategy* takes cognisance of the evolution of how both sport and physical activity are consumed to incorporate a new vision of "lifelong involvement in sport and physical activity leads to an active, healthy, resilient, and inclusive society which recognises and values both participation and excellence" (DfC, 2022, p. 4).

The strategy is underscored by six key themes:

1 Recovery from the Impact of the Pandemic on Sport and Physical Activity
2 Promoting Participation, Inclusion & Community Engagement
3 Promoting Excellence in Sport
4 Promoting Partnership and Integration
5 Providing Inclusive, Shared Spaces and Places
6 Promoting the Benefits of Sport and Physical Activity

The *Active Living Strategy* is underpinned by three cross-cutting principles which recognise the departmental agenda, the draft PfG indicators, and the sectoral need:

1 Developing Inclusive, Shared Communities
2 Developing Capacity and Governance
3 Developing National and International Linkages

The *Active Living Strategy* presents the sport and physical activity continuum (Figure 5.2) throughout the lifespan taking account of pathways, options, and influencing factors.

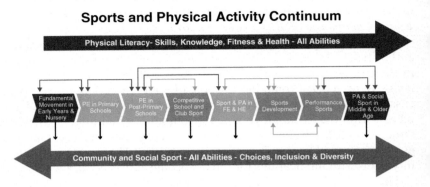

Figure 5.2 Sport and physical activity continuum.

Sport in NI similar to the other UK nations adopts the EU definition of sport established by the Council of Europe which encompasses

> all forms of physical activity which, through casual or organised participation, aim at expressing or improving physical fitness and mental well-being, forming social relationships or obtaining results in competition at all levels.
>
> (COE, 2001)

Although DfC is responsible for the strategic administration and promotion of sport in NI, responsibility for other areas of sport is partitioned across other departments. The cross-departmental relevance of sport is recognised in the diverse use of sport across several government departments. School sport and sporting events are two such examples. Responsibility for school sport is undertaken by the Department for Education (DE), while responsibility for major sporting events is undertaken by the Department for Economy (DfE).

In practice, each department when administrating sports projects should be guided by DfC sports strategy; however, in many cases, these projects, although sports related, are not deemed sports projects and as such will be guided by departmental policies. In essence, how a situation is viewed depends on where you sit (Bogdanor, 2005). The impact on sport can be seen in two situations related to school's sport and sports events. First, the Department of Education recommends that schools offer a minimum of two hours of curricular physical education each week, yet this is not a mandatory requirement of school inspections, thus limiting adherence across the country. Second, the transfer of major sports events to the Department for Economy following the collapse of the NI Events Company in the early 2000s has altered the focus. In recent years, major events such as the British Open (golf) and the Giro d'Italia (cycling) have been hosted in NI in an attempt to promote tourism in NI and attract business to NI, thus ignoring, to some extent, the potential sporting benefits. A further case in point was the Commonwealth Youth Games which the NI Commonwealth Games Council successfully bid for in 2016. With cross-party-political support from Government, Belfast won the right to host the games in 2021, an event which would have been the largest multi-sport event ever to be hosted in NI.

Ultimately, Belfast had to relinquish the right to host the games due to the decision by the Department for Economy (DfE) to not provide the required funding, a decision based on economic viability rather than potential social and sporting benefits. The decision highlights conflicting priorities which prioritise efficiency (Davies, 2009) and economic impact (Flynn, 2012). The absence of sporting criteria in the decision-making criteria is at odds with major sports event planning (Gratton et al., 2005).

It has been suggested that, practically, within the UK the inclusion of sport alongside physical activity and play as a National Lottery good cause and its subsequent introduction within the social inclusion agenda by the Labour UK Government in the late 1990s perpetuated a corresponding shift in UK sports development, from achieving sports-related goals to contributing to Government's broader inclusion objectives (Houlihan & White, 2002).

Elite sport

UK Sport has created a performance model which progresses through organisational culture and sporting culture as a pathway to achieving sporting impact. Nevertheless, the unique circumstances within NI must be considered at a performance sport level. This issue was discussed by Liston et al. (2013) who concluded that although the spreading of sports funding in NI – to promote inclusion – may dilute the ability to achieve Olympic and Paralympic success, NI is a unique country where social benefits must be considered. Indeed, the recent Continuous Household Survey (2019) identified society's positive attitude towards the civic benefits of performance sport, yet wider research calls into question the potential impact of performance sport on social outcomes (Sugden, 2014; Bailey, 2006). This highlights the need for a strong evidence base to underpin sports social benefits.

At an elite level, the establishment of National Institutes of Sports across the four home nations in the early 2000s saw NI create the Sports Institute for NI based at Ulster University's Jordanstown campus. Initially established in partnership with Ulster University, the Institute is now operated solely by SNI providing high-performance sports services to support NI's best athletes and coaches from a central hub.

The stated aim of the high-performance system in NI is to help athletes win medals at World, Olympic/Paralympic, European or Commonwealth Games levels. This goal is achieved through two methods: first, financial investment (Sporting Winners Programme) in about 40 High-Performance Programmes annually, and second, provision of expertise from performance staff including service providers based at the SNISI, with regional satellite provision geographically spread across NI.

Investment in governing bodies of sport either regionally (NI/Ulster) or nationally (GB/Ireland) recognises NI's position at the intersection of both the British and Irish performance sport pathways. The high-performance component of Sport NI's work often focuses on creating a 'springboard' effect to fast-track athletes from NI onto national squads and eventually onto success in international competition. Strategic work with partners Sport Ireland and UK Sport is critical in this regard given NI's unique position regarding sporting pathways.

With a population of approximately 1.9 million people, NI has a relatively small pool of talent from which to identify elite and high-performance athletes. With a global population of around 8 billion and approximately 11,000 of these qualifying for the Olympic Games, in simple terms a population of 1.9 million would be expected to produce around three Olympic athletes. It is therefore of the utmost importance that athletes with potential are not allowed to slip through the net undetected. When SNI committed to take part in the Sport Policy *factors* Leading to International Sporting Success (SPLISS) research in 2014 (Sport NI, 2014), it was concluded that elite sport development systems in NI were 'in their infancy'. Subsequently, SNI has provided the means and direction by which talent identification and development are much more systematic processes, underpinned by the four principles of talent management as shown in Table 5.1.

The effectiveness of these talent identification and development systems can in part be judged by NI's performance in international competition. As a litmus test of the nation's performance, Figure 5.3 shows NI's performance in the Commonwealth Games from 1998 to 2022.

Table 5.1 The Components of the Talent Framework Adopted by Sport NI

1. Planning and Preparation	2. Profiling and Recruitment	3. Talent Confirmation	4. Talent Development
Sport-specific talent plans Intelligence gathering Managing personnel Support services Innovation	Developing sporting profiles Recruiting talent Talent sources Assessment criteria Intakes of talent Geographical searches	Planned programmes Expected benchmarks Progression profiles Transfers within disciplines Transfer across sports	Coaching styles and approaches High performance coaching Regular Continual Professional Development Clearly defined programmes Yearly targets Induction events Monitoring Competition strategy Individual progression mapping

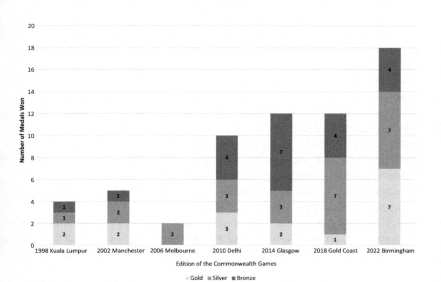

Figure 5.3 Northern Ireland's performance in the Commonwealth Games 1998–2022.

Figure 5.3 shows that between 2010 and 2022 NI won at least ten medals at each Commonwealth Games, which was at least double the total medal wins achieved in the three editions between 1998 and 2006. These data provide some evidence that the processes of talent identification and development have been reasonably successful in contribution to a step change in NI's performances in the Commonwealth Games. With 7 gold medals and 18 medals in total, Birmingham 2022 proved to be NI's best ever Commonwealth Games and provides an indication of how long it takes for an elite sport development system to mature.

Participation and community sport

Sport and physical activity play an important role in government plans to create an active, healthy, resilient, and inclusive society which recognises and values both participation and excellence. *Active Living* recognises the powerful role that sport has to change people's lives for the better. In particular, its potential to bring people together, improve physical and mental health, boost self-esteem and educational attainment, and create a sense of belonging. However, it is also important to recognise that there is a need to remove barriers to lifelong participation in sport and physical activity by creating environments that provide more opportunities to participate and to have fun, and are welcoming to all including people with a disability, older people, women and girls, people living in areas of high social need, and those from new and settled migrant communities (Department for Communities, 2022).

As mentioned previously, *Active Living* seeks to build on the successes of *Sports Matters – The Northern Ireland Strategy for Sport & Physical Recreation 2009–2019* (Department for Communities, 2009). Having focused on the 3Ps of Participation, Performance, and Places within Sport Matters, a strategic monitoring group (policy stakeholders) and strategic implementation group (operations stakeholders) demonstrated how 25/26 key outputs were achieved supported by data from Northern Ireland Statistics and Research Agency and Continuous Household Survey (CHS).

Active Living progresses to create a new strategic framework that is based around inclusion, engagement, community excellence, partnership, and shared spaces that collectively maximise the benefits of more people, being more active, more of the time. It reflects the significant impact the COVID-19 pandemic has had, and will continue to have, on society and the importance of ensuring that there is a strong focus on recovery, including the role sport and physical activity must play in managing the physical and mental health challenges that the COVID-19 pandemic has created (Sport NI, 2021). This includes the importance of key stakeholders such as government departments, arm's length bodies, local councils, governing bodies of sport, and others working with and supporting each other to support the sector, build capacity, capability, and resilience.

Active Living further acknowledges the importance of a number of fundamental 'foundation blocks', outlined in Figure 5.4, that will be used to support the successful implementation of strategy including its agreed vision, themes, goals, and cross-cutting principles over the next ten years or more. Community-based sport and physical activity is one of the central blocks considered and recognised within the strategy as the space within which many benefits can be realised such as building community cohesion within local communities, improving social interaction, and contributing to the health and well-being of participants.

The most authoritative data currently available on adult demand for participation in sport and physical activity in NI is the CHS. The CHS has been in place since 1983 and routinely includes questions on sport and leisure. To put the challenge of getting more adults, more active, more of the time in NI into context, it is worth examining the broader picture of participation rates across all forms of sport and physical activity measured by the CHS. Figure 5.5 provides an analysis of all the sports and activities reported in 2019/2020.

Although not shown in Figure 5.5, just under half (49%) of adults in NI take part in recreational walking, which is by far the most popular physical activity amongst adults in NI. If more vigorous and more 'sporty' activities are examined, then keepfit, aerobics, yoga, and

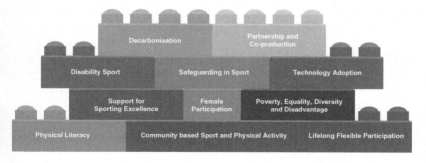

Figure 5.4 Foundation blocks for the *Active Living Strategy*.
Source: Department for Communities (2022), p. 20.

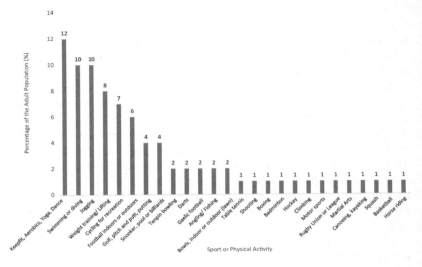

Figure 5.5 Participation rates in the most popular sports and activities in Northern Ireland – adults (16+ years)

dance exercises combined are next most popular activities with a participation rate of 12%, followed by swimming and jogging (both 10%). These findings point to the increasing trend of solo lifestyle activities being more popular than team sports such as football (6%).

Children and young people

Similarly, the most authoritative data currently available on children and young people's demand for participation in sport and physical activity in NI is the Children's Sport Participation and Physical Activity (CSPPA 2018) study (Woods et al., 2019). CSPPA 2018 was a follow-up to CSPPA 2010 (Woods et al., 2010) to investigate physical activity, sports participation, and PE amongst children and adolescents (aged 10–18 years) across the island of Ireland. In total, 6,651 children aged 10–18 took part in the CSPPA 2018 study from across the island of Ireland, with 1954 primary and post-primary students making up the NI sample. In order to achieve a representative sample, all mainstream primary and post-primary schools from NI were included in the sampling frame. Schools were stratified by four criteria: school gender (male, female, or mixed), school location (urban or rural, categorised by population density), and size (small, medium, or large, based on the total number of pupils) and socio-economic status (high, medium, low). A total of 51 schools were contacted (20 primary and 31 post-primary) to ensure an equivalent sample to the Republic of Ireland sample and 29 schools, 3% of all schools (9 primary and 20 post-primary), was recruited. Primary (including Year 6 and Year 7/age 10–11 years) and post-primary (Year 8–Year 14/age 12–18 years) pupils completed the survey between March and June 2018. As with adults, it is also worth examining the broader picture of participation rates of children and young people from a community sport (i.e., outside the school setting) perspective and the range of community sport activities that pupils reported being engaged in to highlight some of challenges that stakeholders will need to collectively address over the next decade and beyond through the implementation of *Active Living*.

Table 5.2 shows the frequency of community sport participation (i.e., outside of school) for primary and post-primary school children. At primary school level, 65% of pupils reported participating in community sport at least once a week, with 49% of post-primary school pupils reporting participation at least once a week. Fourteen percent of primary and 47% post-primary school pupils reported never participating in community sport (Table 5.2). At post-primary school level, the numbers of those who reported never participating in community sport appeared to be a significant issue. Sport is measured in terms of participation rates, membership of clubs, and creation of new clubs.

The range of school sports for primary and post-primary school pupils is presented in Table 5.3. Soccer, basketball, rugby, Gaelic football, and swimming or athletics were the most popular school sports

Table 5.2 Community Sport Participation for Primary and Post-Primary School Pupils

Frequency	Primary School Primary pupils %	Post-Primary School Post-primary pupils %
Four or more days a week	13	18
Two to three days a week	31	22
One day a week	21	8
Less often	21	5
Never	14	47

Table 5.3 Most Popular Community Sports for Primary and Post-Primary School Pupils Combined over the Last 12 Months

	Combined Primary and Post-Primary Schools		
Sport/Activity	Boys %	Girls %	All %
Adventure activities	5	5	5
Aerobics/exercise class	1	2	1
Athletics	7	11	9
Badminton	3	15	4
Baseball/rounders	2	5	3
Basketball	7	5	6
Camogie	1	6	3
Cross-country running	6	5	8
Dance	2	9	11
Gaelic football	13	20	11
Golf	1	9	1
Gymnastics	2	1	9
Handball	3	16	3
Hockey	3	4	10
Horse riding	3	16	6
Hurling	7	8	4
Martial arts	7	2	6
Netball	0	5	1
Rugby	14	4	9
Soccer	34	10	22
Squash	2	2	2
Surfing	4	2	3
Swimming	13	18	16
Tennis	6	7	7
Triathlon	2	1	1
Volleyball	3	4	3
Weight training	9	6	7

for boys, whereas hockey, soccer, dance, basketball, athletics, cross country, and gymnastics were the most popular girls' sports. Boys favoured team sports with girls having a combination of team and individual sports.

PE and school sport

Responsibility for schools and school sport sits under the DE, operationalised through the Education Authority. The curriculum, examinations, and assessment are the responsibility of the Council for the Curriculum, Examinations and Assessment (CCEA) a non-departmental public body (NDPB) funded by and responsible to the Department of Education (DE).

Physical education (PE) is a compulsory activity in the NI curriculum for all children aged 4–16. Primary school children take part in activities at the foundation stage. Key stage 1 offers athletics, dance, games, and gymnastics, while key stages 2 and 3 also include swimming. These activities develop from fundamental movement skills (balance, coordination, control locomotion, and manipulation) to building social skills, confidence, and respect while understanding the benefits of being active and healthy. Key stage 4 supports students to plan and participate in a balanced programme of PE (Delaney, 2008).

While PE is a compulsory part of the curriculum, the Education Authority guidance recommends the provision of a minimum of two hours of curricular PE per week across key stages 1–4 it is, however, each school that have responsibility for delivery and thus provision can fluctuate depending on priorities. The Children's Sport Participation and Physical Activity (CSPPA) study found that the majority of schools in NI are not meeting the two hours' guidance, with only 40% of post-primary pupils receiving the minimum recommended level (Connelly et al., 2020). The absence of a legal requirement to meet a minimum PE guideline restricts the ability to improve adherence as schools face competing priorities and scrutiny of outcomes (Connelly et al., 2020). Unlike secondary schools in NI, Primary schools do not have specialist PE teachers and thus rely on generalist teachers who have limited in service training on PE.

The NI government recognise the importance of people being active, for example, outcome four within the Draft Programme for Government states "We enjoy long, healthy, active lives" (The Executive Office, n.d.); as a result, all departments have a role to play in sport and addressing the concerning levels of inactivity across NI, which indicates only 13% of school children in NI met the guidelines of 60 minutes of physical activity per day, with a progressive decline in physical activity from primary school (20%) to secondary school (11%) (Woods et al, 2019).

Physical literacy

In the early 2000s, SNI integrated the concept of physical literacy and its delivery into policy and programmes across Northern Ireland (SNI, 2005). In 2009, SNI and Sport Ireland collaborated to establish the Lifelong Involvement in Sport and Physical Activity (LISPA) model as a conceptual framework for sports development planning. Physical literacy embraces the view that participation in sport and physical activity over the life course includes preschool children, school-going children, and adults of all ages, which is recognised in the (LISPA) framework (Delaney, 2008).

Physical literacy is an evolving concept; as such its adoption is dependent on interpretations. Therefore, countries such as Canada, Australia, and, most recently, the island of Ireland (NI and Ireland) launched a national physical literacy statement. This contextualised definition aims to support the future cross-sectoral implementation of physical literacy.

> Physical literacy is the motivation, confidence, physical competence, knowledge and understanding that enables a person to value and participate in physical activity throughout life.
>
> (Sport Ireland, 2022, p. 1)

The statement further identifies that physical literacy necessitates the development of three interconnected learning domains (cognitive, affective, and physical).

Government strategies have identified physical literacy as having a role to play in building active populations (*Children and Young People's Strategy 2020*), and in particular, the *Active Living Strategy 2022* describes how

> embracing physical literacy, fundamental movement skills and physical activity from a young age with a focus on lifelong involvement in sport and physical activity, are key building blocks for the strategy and will ensure people are active into old age.
>
> (Department for Communities, p. 12)

At a practical level, curriculum school sport and PE is supported with a range of programmes and investments both in curriculum time (Curriculum Sports Programme and the Daily) and beyond (Active School Travel and Extended Schools). These examples amongst others demonstrate the growth of a systems approach building partnership at both national and local levels to achieve outcomes for children through sport and physical activity.

The Curriculum Sports Programme (CSP)

The Department of Education introduced in the CSP in 2007 with the target of developing fundamental movement skills (initially with key stage 1 pupils before a refocus on key stage 2 in 2019) delivered by governing body coaches from the Irish Football Association (IFA) and Gaelic Athletic Association (GAA). These coaches were trained in specific early years physical literacy skills, integrating cross-curricular themes and healthy lifestyle messages through physical literacy to raise the confidence and self-esteem of pupils while building confidence of teachers in PE delivery (Irish Football Association, 2015). This was the first official PE programme in schools to be delivered by non-qualified teachers and reflected a move towards delivering broader sport in the community programmes within schools (Woods et al., 2010) which has seen a number of governing bodies deliver coaching sessions within the school setting and provide support to schools in the organisation of competitive sports programmes.

The Daily Mile

The Daily Mile encourages schools to take children outside for a 15-minute run, jog, or walk every day designed to promote mental health and well-being. This is a voluntary activity (established initially in Scotland), with individual schools participating when it best suits their schedule. Recent studies demonstrating improved health measures for those taking part compared to peers with greater levels of fitness, lower levels of body fat, and reduced sedentary behaviour (Moran et al., 2019).

The Active School Travel programme

The Department for Infrastructure and the Public Health Agency fund the Active School Travel programme to facilitate increased walking and cycling as part of travel to and from school by providing a range of activities which are supported by a Sustrans. In 2021, the programme saw an increase of just over 10% in the number of children travelling actively to school at participating schools, which led to an increase from 26% to 41% in the number of children completing physical activity for at least 60 minutes each day (Sustrans, 2021).

Extended Schools

The Extended Schools programme primarily targets schools with high numbers of pupils with free school meal entitlement providing sport and play activities before, during, and after school as well as during school holidays. Funding is available to support teacher-led activities as well as community and sporting groups to promote healthy lifestyles. Research shows that just over 90% of schools involved documented evidence that Extended Schools is fostering health and well-being (Department for Education, 2019).

School sport across NI has demonstrated a transition towards adopting further collaborative community-based approaches to tackle a broader societal issue related to inactivity by using various programmes and messaging to promote the need for healthy lifestyles underpinned by physical literacy.

Sport development programmes and policies

In recent years, the Department for Communities and Sport NI have invested in a range of programmes to promote participation and break down barriers to under-represented groups. Examples include *Everybody Active, Active Living: No Limits,* and *Active Women and Girls: Active, Fit and Sporty.*

Every Body Active

Every Body Active attempted to get people more active more often through sport and physical activity in NI as part of a lottery funded programme delivered in conjunction with the 11 district councils. The programme provided opportunities across a wide range of sports and activities through collaborations involving clubs, schools, and community organisations targeting under-represented groups with the aim of increasing participation in sport and physical activity across key life course transitions from school through to retirement.

Active Living: No Limits

Active Living: No Limits focuses on improving the health and well-being of people with a disability in NI through a collaborative approach to increase participation in sport and active recreation (Sport NI, 2016). The collaborative nature of this programme brought delivery and policy stakeholders together with end users to share information and better understand each other, creating an action plan to address identified issues. The programme involved giving direction to the development of disability sport across NI, by encouraging strategic and joined up working towards an agreed direction for strategic investment in disability sport. The action plan not only contributed towards the sport-specific strategy but also cross-departmental outcome-focused strategies including *NI Executive: A Strategy to improve the lives of people with disabilities (2012–2017)*, the Department of Health's *Physical and Sensory Disability Strategy and Action Plan (2012–2015)*, *Northern Ireland Executive: Active Ageing Strategy (2016–2021)*, and *Children with Disabilities Strategic Alliance: Children and Young People Manifesto (2012)*. A range of projects were delivered which reduced barriers to participation, provided adopted equipment, developed a network of multisport hubs, increased training opportunities, built capacity, raised awareness, and challenged misconceptions.

Active Fit and Sporty

The Women and Girls: Active, Fit and Sporty strategic framework supported a number of sports clubs and community groups to deliver a range of sporting opportunities for women and girls by tackling barriers and building local partnerships. The objective was to increase the number of women and girls participating in sport and physical activity through campaigns and projects across four key elements: media, leadership, role models, and research and evaluation (Sport NI, 2019).

Challenges and barriers to sport development

Identity issues in NI are made more ambiguous by the presence of two communities (Protestant and Catholic), which engender a low collective identification (Gormley-Heenan & Aughey, 2017) towards an inclusive national identity. On one side, the existence of British symbols (anthem and flags) are perceived as excluding the Irish cultural identity, while on the other, calls for their removal are seen as further evidence of the erosion of the British cultural identity (Hassan & Ferguson, 2019). Sport is one of the few mechanisms for the public expression of identity in shared spaces, yet politico-religious markers (Mitchell et al., 2016) perpetuate the perceived politicised relationship between identity and sport. This creates a challenge for athletes with regard to representation, for administrators in terms of governance, and for funders in relation to parity. Fans also face barriers with some reluctant to visit venues associated with the 'other side' contributing to the perception of exclusion.

Financial constraints are also significant. With a budget of less than £30 million per year, SNI must deliver on both participation and performance outcomes, which has major implications to potential success at an elite level, particularly when we consider the perceived cost of winning a gold medal at an Olympic games to be just over

£4 million (Sports Management, 2016). Moreover, the overarching sporting policy in NI prioritises a community focus (Donnelly et al., 2015). Consequently, any sports performance policy in NI is required to demonstrate cultural impact towards government outcomes. The unique situation requiring funding to be equitably spread in accordance with the 'parity of esteem' principle even if this might dilute the ability to achieve World, Olympic, or Paralympic success.

The impact of the multi-layers of governance across the political environment in NI (Birrell, 2014) can be viewed through the diversity of funding sources for the third sector in general and sport-related activity in particular in NI. This has resulted in an increase in funding for sport-related activities distributed by non-sport-focused organisations at the same time as a substantial reduction in funding for traditional sports development programming. The increasingly diverse availability of funding in NI places pressure on sporting bodies to move beyond traditional sports development programmes towards the delivery of inclusion and sport for development activities. The management of these sport-related projects continues to be shaped by the neoliberal value for money ethos, which concentrates on clearly defined project-level outcomes. The result is to limit collaborations by prioritising value for money criteria and quantitative-based monitoring criteria resulting in a prevalence of tasked based projects. The absence of a population-level evaluation model further restricts the ability of the sport sector to demonstrate value and thus take control of its future strategic direction.

Summary

This chapter has reviewed the unique contextual factors which instigate the complex public sector and sporting structures in Northern Ireland. Particular attention was paid to the dual Olympic sporting pathway available to athletes in Northern Ireland and the relative impact this has on sports policy at a performance level. The draft NI Programme for Government (2016 and 2021) has transitioned policy in NI towards an outcomes-based framework which has been embedded within *Active Living Strategy 2022*. This strategy for the first time expands the reach of sport to include physical activity and encourages stakeholders to collaborate across a range of agendas to achieve sporting benefits. Nevertheless, statutory responsibility for sport is separated across different government departments for areas such as school sports, sports events, sports development, elite sport, and sport for development. The inclusion of a particularly specific sport-related indicator within the Programme for Government therefore promotes the ability to effectively collaborate, reducing the risk of unregulated activity and duplication. Future research should focus on the measurement of sport and physical activity benefits across NI at an organisational performance and population level.

References

Adams, A. and Harris, K. (2014). Making sense of the lack of evidence discourse, power and knowledge in the field of sport for development. *International Journal of Public Sector Management*, 27(2), 140–151.

Bailey, R. (2006). Physical education and sport in schools: A review of benefits and outcomes. *Journal of School Health*, 76(8), 397–401.

Bairner, A. (2013). Sport, the Northern Ireland peace process, and the politics of identity. *Journal of Aggression, Conflict and Peace Research*, 5(4), 220–229.

Birrell, D. (2014). Qualitative research and policy-making in Northern Ireland: barriers arising from the lack of consensus, capacity and conceptualization. *Innovation: The European Journal of Social Science Research*, 27(1), 20–30.

Bogdanor, V. (Ed.), (2005). *Joined-up government* (Vol. 5). Oxford University Press.

Bush, K., & Houston, K. (2012). *The story of peace learning from the EU Peace funding in Northern Ireland and the border region*. Incore.

Coalter, F. (2009). Sport-in-development: Accountability or development? In R. Levermore and A. Beacom. (Eds.). *Sport and international development* (pp. 55–76). Palgrave MacMillan.

Council of Europe. (2001). Recommendation No. R (92) 13 REV of the Committee of Ministers to Member States on the Revised European Sports Charter. Available at: https://rm.coe.int/16804c9dbb [Accessed August 2017].

Davies, J. S. (2009). The limits of joined-up government: Towards a political analysis. *Public Administration*, 87(1), 80–96.

Delaney, B. J., Donnelly, P., News, J., & Haughey, T. J. (2008). Improving physical literacy: A review of current practice and literature relating to the development, delivery and measurement of physical literacy with recommendations for further action. Available from: https://pure.ulster.ac.uk/ws/portalfiles/portal/91095874/ImprovingPhysicalLiteracy_SNI_PDF_MARCH_08.pdf

Department for Communities. (2009). The Northern Ireland Strategy for Sport and Physical Recreation 2009 to 2019. Available at: https://www.communities-ni.gov.uk/sites/default/files/The-northern-ireland-strategy-for-sport-and-physical-recreation-2009-2019.pdf

Department for Communities. (2022). Sport and Physical Activity Strategy NI. Available at: https://www.communities-ni.gov.uk/sites/default/files/

publications/communities/dfc-active-living-sport-physical-strategy-northern-ireland.pdf.

Donnelly, P., Shibli, S., & Toole, S. (2015). Sports Clubs in Northern Ireland. In C. Breuer., R. Hoekman., S. Nagel, & van der Werff, H., (Eds.). *Sport clubs in Europe* (pp. 291–308). Springer.

Ferguson, K. Hassan, D., & Kitchin, P. (2017). Sport and underachievement amongst protestant youth in Northern Ireland: A boxing club case study. *International Journal of Sport Policy and Politics, 34*, 1–45.

Flynn, R. (2012). *Structures of control in health management.* Routledge.

Friedman, M. (2005). *The optimum quantity of money.* Transaction Publishers.

Gratton, C., Shibli, S., & Coleman, R. (2005). Sport and economic regeneration in cities. *Urban Studies, 42*(5–6), 985–999.

Gormley-Heenan, C., & Aughey, A. (2017). Northern Ireland and Brexit: Three effects on 'the border in the mind'. *The British Journal of Politics and International Relations, 19*(3), 497–511.

Hassan, D., & Ferguson, K. (2019). Still as divided as ever? Northern Ireland, football and identity 20 years after the Good Friday Agreement. *Soccer & Society, 20*(7–8), 1071–1083.

Haase, D. (2018). The Economic, Social and Territorial Situation of Northern Ireland. European Parliament. Available at: http://www.europarl.europa.eu/RegData/etudes/IDAN/2018/617459/IPOL_IDA(2018)617459_EN.pdf [Accessed May 2019].

Houlihan, B. (1997). Sport, national identity and public policy. *Nations and Nationalism, 3*(1), 113–137.

Houlihan, B., & White, A. (2002). *The politics of sports development.* Routledge.

Huntley, D. (1988). An analysis of leisure centre provision in Belfast. Unpublished BA Hons (Sports Studies) dissertation, University of Ulster, Jordanstown.

Irish Football Association. (2015). Curriculum Sports Programme 2015 [online]. Available at: https://www.irishfa.com/media/7207/curriculum-sports-programme-end-of-year-report-july-2015.pdf.

Liston, K., Gregg, R., & Lowther, J. (2013). Elite sports policy and coaching at the coalface. *International Journal of Sport Policy and Politics, 5*(3), 341–362.

Mitchell, P., Somerville, I., & Hargie, O. (2016). Sport for peace in Northern Ireland? Civil society, change and constraint after the 1998 Good Friday Agreement. *The British Journal of Politics and International Relations, 23*(1), 34–49.

Moran, C., Brooks, N., Booth, J., Chesham, R., Sweeney, E., Ryde, G., & Gorely, T. (2019). *The impact of the Daily Mile on primary school children.* University of Stirling. https://www.stir.ac.uk/research/public-policy-hub/policy-briefings/.

Sport Ireland. (2022). All Island Physical Literacy Statement. Available at: www.sportireland.ie/sites/default/files/media/document/2022-10/Physical%20Literacy%20Statement.pdf.

Sport NI. (2014). Sport Policy *factors* Leading to International Sporting Success (SPLISS). Available at: Splissreducedwebversion.pdf (sportni.net).

Sport NI. (2016). Active Living: No Limits. Available at: http://www.sportni.net/wp-content/uploads/2016/10/Active-Living-No-Limits-Action-Plan-2016-2021.pdf.

Sport NI. (2019). The Women and Girls: Active, Fit and Sporty Participation Survey 2019 Insight Report. Available at: http://www.sportni.net/wp-content/uploads/2020/02/SportNi-Participation-in-Sport-doc_web.pdf.

Sport NI. (2021). Project Re Boot. Available at: www.sportni.net/wp-content/uploads/2021/02/Project-Re-Boot-Team-Up-what-the-evidence-tells-us1.pdf.

Sports Council. (2017). UK Sports Councils' Recognition Policy. Available at: https://sportscotland.org.uk/media/2642/uk-recognition-policy-2017-final-for-publication.pdf.

Sports Management. (2016). Rio 2016 Olympics 20(15) no 127, 44–45. Available at: https://www.sportsmanagement.co.uk/digital/index1.cfm?mag=Sports%20Management&codeid=31317&linktype=story&ref=n&issue=Sep%20Oct%202017%20issue%20133.

Sugden, J. (2010). Critical left-realism and sport interventions in divided societies. *International Review for the Sociology of Sport, 45*(3), 258–272.

Sugden, J. (2014). *Sport and peace-building in divided societies: Playing with the enemy*. Routledge.

Sustrans. (2021). Getting Children Active on the School Run: Active School Travel Programme 2020–21 Summary Report. Available at: https://www.sustrans.org.uk/media/9757/ni-ast-2020-21-summary-report.pdf.

The Executive Office. (n.d.). We All Enjoy Long, Healthy, Active Lives. Available at: https://www.executiveoffice-ni.gov.uk/outcomes/we-all-enjoy-long-healthy-active-lives

Woods, C., Powell, C., Saunders, J. A., O'Brien, W., Murphy, M. H., Duff, C., Farmer, O., Johnston, A., Connolly, S., & Belton, S. (2019). The Children's Sport Participation and Physical Activity Study 2018 (CSPPA 2018).

Woods, C. B., Tannehill, D., Quinlan, A., Moyna, N., & Walsh, J. (2010). The Children's Sport Participation and Physical Activity Study (CSPPA Study).

6 Conclusion

Mathew Dowling, Spencer Harris, and Chris Mackintosh

Introduction

The purpose of this final chapter is to identify common trends and general themes that can be drawn from each of the four home nation case studies. At this point, it is worth reminding the reader that our overall intention of this study was to provide an in-depth analysis of sport policy within each home nation and to identify similarities and differences across the home nations in order to generate broader inferences about the nature and complexities of sport policy across the UK. The chapter begins with a discussion of general themes and observations about the evolution of sport policy across each of the four home nation chapters. We re-emphasise our original definition of the policy process as one by which choices are bounded by rational and irrational shortcuts instigated by policy and decision-makers, who in turn are influenced by key elements of the policy environment (i.e., institutional norms, networks, the importance of ideas and beliefs, policy conditions, and key focusing events) (Cairney, 2019 – see chapter 1). The purpose of drawing upon Cairney's conceptualisation here is not to deductively apply *all* elements of the policy process to each home nation case, but rather to enable a more holistic and nuanced understanding of the nature and complexities of the sport policy process across the UK. We utilise the analytical framework outlined previously (Figure 1.1) to guide our analysis and to provide a degree of consistency – or functional equivalence (Dowling & Harris, 2021) – to enable comparisons to be made between each of the home nation cases. Within this section, we look back across the four home country chapters to identify common trends, patterns, and specific areas where policies, processes, and practices either converge or diverge across the cases. The final part of the chapter reflects upon the methodological limitations and considers potential future research directions.

DOI: 10.4324/9781003241232-6

Evolution of sport policy

This section reflects upon the evolution of sport policy across the home nations. Our analysis identified four themes: (1) *devolution*, (2) *the dominance of Westminster in policy and decision-making*, (3) *increasing jurisdictional overlap*, and (4) *policy convergence of key priorities and outcomes* across the home nations. Each of these themes will be discussed in turn.

Devolution

The first theme that can be drawn from the cases is that devolution has been a dominant force in shaping a new sport policy discourse oriented more towards the needs and peculiarities of each home country. Consistent with Cairney's (2019) conceptualisation that the nature and structure of policy environment is continually influenced by contextual factors, we can see clear evidence from cases that sport policy is moulded by the historical, cultural, and geographical context of each home country. In Northern Ireland, for example, the Good Friday/Belfast Agreement of 1998 sees the country emerging from a 30-year period of conflict into a service-led economy where sport tourism is a hub of activity. The Northern Ireland chapter also reveals the importance of landmark historical events such as the partition the period of troubles, the post-conflict Good Friday Agreement in the devolution process as well as the criticality of the National Lottery and the national reform of public administration to the Northern Irish sport policy process. For Wales, the combination of their comparatively successful elite sport programme and their hosting of several high-profile, mega-sport events carries symbolic and practical importance. These developments reflect the Welsh desire to emulate a nation that is renowned for its commitment to sport – one that, as a small nation, punches well above its weight as well as demonstrating its ability to produce high-performance success. Additionally, new policy institutions such as Public Health Wales and Natural Resource Wales have emerged alongside the long-established Welsh Sports Council (Sport Wales) and Welsh NGBs of sport. These institutions have helped to broaden a devolved Welsh sports policy to use community sport as a vehicle to achieve health and well-being goals as well as retaining a focus on sporting excellence. Scotland's sport policy process is primarily driven by the Scottish Parliament in close partnership with the Scottish Sport Council (Sport Scotland). Local government and National Governing Bodies of Sport (NGBs), alongside a collective of other national and sub-regional agencies, run and manage the implementation of national policy. Further, sport in Scotland has featured as an important aspect of recent political party manifestos, with parties focusing on a variety of issues such as health and well-being, equity, facilities, mass sport participation, and outdoor recreation.

Devolution has also triggered some important differences in how the home nations have responded to their new powers and structures. All four cases identified unique social, historical, and political contextual factors which have influenced how sport and physical activity is organised and delivered. Specifically, the cases reveal key differences in the *focusing events* that were identified as significant to the evolution of sport policy. In England, the *Wolfenden Report* and its key recommendations to provide public funding and establish an advisory sport council (which later became the English Sport Council in 1972) were significant for (re)organising sport in the county, as well as having a significant impact on, and had far wider reaching implications for, the evolution of sport policy across the other home nations. For example, the establishment of the English Sports Council provided an impetus for establishing sports councils in Scotland (1971) and Wales (1972), respectively. In Scotland, devolution provided a highly desired opportunity for greater independence in sporting matters, with many sport policy matters now being determined by the Holyrood Parliament and *sportscotland*. In Wales, the broader forces of marketisation and privatisation and the 1997 general election and referendum were significant influences on the development of Welsh sport policy. The influence of contextual factors and key focusing events on the evolution of sport policy was perhaps most evident in the Northern Ireland case. Here, the authors put significant emphasis on the influence of broader social and political events (e.g., the partition, the troubles, Belfast Agreement). The Belfast Agreement in 1998 was particularly significant for elite sport as it enshrined the rights of athletes in NI to compete for Ireland, GB, or NI in international competition. These structural factors and their wide-reaching influence from one home nation to the next also reveal the extent to which much of the sport policymaking process is beyond the control of policy- and decision-makers within their respective countries. Nonetheless, the impact of these English-based developments on other home nations is also indicative of our next theme – the continued dominance of Westminster across the home nations.

Westminster/English policy dominance

A second theme from the study is strong evidence to suggest that Westminster has historically dominated sport policy, to

Conclusion 111

varying degrees, across each of the home nations, influencing both decision-making processes and agenda setting. Examples include (1) the ongoing influence of the English sports councils (and UK Sport in particular) who have been key actors in creating and maintaining the institutional and structural arrangements across many home nations. This is often enacted through pre-existing funding mechanisms and the creation of UK-wide programmes such as the National Junior Sports Programme, the UK Coaching Framework, and the home country National Institutes of Sport for example; (2) the role and influence of existing and new legislation and reforms (e.g. Education Reform Act and Compulsory Competitive Tendering) from England that has impacted home nations; and (3) the historical importance of English-based focus events/developments (e.g. establishment of the National Lottery and English sport council) for the evolution of sport policy within Scotland, Wales, and, to a lesser extent, Northern Ireland. We even see evidence of Westminster dominance in the nature and composition of the home nation chapters within this study. Within the England chapter, the evolution of the sport policy process is well documented (see, e.g., Bloyce & Smith, 2010; Houlihan, 1997; Houlihan & Lindsey, 2013; Houlihan & White, 2002), but our reading of the other home chapters, and evidence from our own systematic review of the literature (see Appendix 2), suggests that the evolution of sport policy is less well documented within other home nations. Not only does this finding lend further support for the initial rationale for this study but also highlights the need to further document the nature and evolution of sport policy within each of the home nations respectively (see section *methodological reflections and future directions* for a more detailed discussion here).

The above examples also suggest that despite the ongoing process of devolution and the devolvement of power to the government ministries and governing agencies, Westminster continues to dominate sport policy and decision-making processes through the ongoing process of devolution. In this sense, despite the rhetoric of devolution, we see evidence to suggest that sport policy across the UK remains heavily influenced by Westminster, with power predominantly remaining in Whitehall. This finding is consistent with Marsh et al.'s (2003) conceptualisation of the British political system being characterised by structural inequalities, unequal power relations, and a constrained but not hollowed out state which maintains a strong but segmented core executive. With that said, we are equally mindful of Cairney's (2019) remarks that the power of the centre (i.e., government) is limited and that the "assumption of centralization would also be a big mistake empirically because formal sources of power are concentrated but actual power to make and influence policy is dispersed widely across political systems" (p. 7). In support of Cairney's viewpoint, we also see numerous examples for how some home countries are diverging from the DCMS policy and UK-wide visions and policies, specifically in sport policy areas not bound by UK or GB requirements (i.e., school sport, community sport programming). This suggests that despite formal authority and power often residing with government (vis-à-vis DCMS) and governmental agencies (vis-à-vis UK Sport) in England that structural arrangements are shifting, and that power is increasingly dispersed across the home nations. Furthermore, as these changes in structural arrangements normalise over time, it will be interesting to examine the extent to which the DCMS – despite retaining its influence through funding control – is able to continue to exert control and govern three administratively and geographical dispersed sport policymaking bodies.

Increasing jurisdictional overlap and stakeholder involvement

A third theme that can be drawn from our analysis of the four home nation cases is that the sporting *networks and administrative arrangements* across the home nations are complex, representing an increasingly "crowded policy space" (Houlihan, 2000, p. 181). This is primarily due to the jurisdictional overlap in the roles and responsibilities of key stakeholders but also in relation to the number of stakeholders involved in policy- and decision-making processes across the home nation and the UK. In terms of jurisdictional overlap, the England chapter argues that it is "especially difficult" to examine sport policy in England in isolation from other home nations. The authors go on to directly quote the DCMS/Strategy Unit by stating that "it is not possible to undertake a review of English sports policy, structures and systems without considering the wider UK position" (p. 21). What can be drawn from the other home nation cases and the above discussion regarding the dominance of Westminster is that the opposite also holds – that it is not possible to understand the evolution of sport policy within each of the home nations without considering the role and influence of England. This is apparent when reflecting on the discussion of sport policy in the home nations, which focused on the influence of England-based developments or more contemporary sport policies/strategies within their respective nations. Both instances demonstrate the inherent overlap in the evolution of sport policy across home nations and the difficulty in being able to disentangle the interconnected nature of sport policy between the home nations. Nonetheless, it is the very nature of these policy overlaps and inherent complexities of the sport policymaking process within and across the home nations – and the need to further understand jurisdictional responsibilities – that partly influenced our initial interest in conducting this study. It is also for this reason that the timing of this study is perhaps not coincidental in that there has been sufficient time for the process of devolution to 'gather pace' to enable at least a degree of policy divergence of select home nations from England to warrant a study of this kind.

The home nation cases also suggest that the overlap of roles and responsibilities is often confusing and ambiguous, particularly in relation to who was responsible for elite sport provision. This is likely due to the continued influence of UK Sport which retains responsibility for elite sport across the UK. Consequently, there is a strong degree of convergence in relation to elite sport structures, with many athletes funded through the same (or similar) world-class pathways and with training and support coordinated by decentralised elite sport institutes. However, home nation sports councils also retain responsibility for the development of elite sport within their own country in line with the requirement of certain sport-specific arrangements (e.g., football, cricket, rugby) as well as home nation teams for the Commonwealth Games.

In terms of governing structures and networks in the home nations, all authors used similar terminology such as "complex" and "fragmented" to describe their own contexts, but interestingly none of the authors in the present study elaborated further on what they meant by these terms. Again, this use of terminology is consistent with Cairney's (2019) conceptualisation of policymaking as "complex, messy, and often appears to be unpredictable" (p. 4) and that policy networks and subsystems are pervasive and that a wide range of actors are increasingly influencing policymaking across various levels of government. Both findings (i.e., increased jurisdictional overlap and stakeholder involvement) are also indicative of the increasingly blurred boundaries between the state and civil society and the broader shift from government to governance (Rhodes, 1997).

Broader policy shifts: policy convergence and change

A fourth theme is the apparent policy convergence of key priorities and outcomes across the home nations. Here, even despite devolution and some degree of divergence of approach, we also see many similarities with regard to policy direction and outcomes across the cases. The first observation that can be drawn from our cases is a general shift in UK sport policy from sport for sport to sport for good agenda (primarily health). More specifically, in terms of policy priorities, all home nations seem to place a greater emphasis on 'sport for sport sake' in the lead up to, and hosting of, the London 2012 Olympic Games. It is clear from the cases that the event itself and the developments leading up to it had a significant impact on the development of sport policy within home nations and across the UK. In addition, the England and Wales home nation cases highlight the inherent uneasiness and potential conflicts and challenges that may arise with governing agencies (e.g., Sport England, Sport Wales) moving away from the traditional domain of sport towards a broader health and physical activity focus. Similar arguments have also been made by Dowling (2021) with regard to Sport England's latest strategy, *Uniting the Movement*. A second observation is that these contemporary sporting strategies/policies also seem to be adopting longer-term approaches (typically 10–20 years). The Welsh Government's current strategy, *Climbing Higher*, is a 20-year strategy for sport and physical activity. England has recently seen the publication and implementation of Sport England's *Uniting the Movement* – a ten-year strategy for sport and physical activity. Interestingly, the home nation cases all recognised the inherent tensions between elite and community sport (i.e., the so-called 'mass–elite dilemma') – in terms of both investment and political priorities, with that latter often dictating the former – although the degree to which this tension is evident differed across cases.

The next sections provide a more detailed discussion of the insights that can be drawn from the cases in relation to elite, community, and physical education/school sport, sport development programmes, and challenges and barriers to sport development provision.

Elite sport

As a UK-wide body, UK Sport remains influential and ultimately retains responsibility for creating an overarching agenda across the UK alongside home nations which also now hold responsibility for talent identification and development. Much of UK Sport's authority stems from its ability to directly support athletes through its world-class pathway funding programme, with the day-to-day training and support being delivered through the decentralised elite sport institutes. Decentralised national training centres for elite sport are present across all home nations. Many of these centres form part of a wider regional network of centres for elite support. In England, UK Sport directly funds the English Institute of Sport and parallel

Conclusion 115

system for World Class Podium, World Class Podium Potential, and Performance Foundations, whereas the Scottish Institute of Sport (SIS), Sport Northern Ireland Sports Institute (SNISI) and Welsh Institute of Sport (WIS) are all owned and managed by the respective home nation Sport Council. National centres are also operating in each home nation in partnership with various facilities and organisations.

The cases also show how elite sport is closely related to national culture and identity. This was particularly evident in Scotland and Wales, but also apparent in Northern Ireland and England. England, Scotland, and Wales have also developed a serious commitment to hosting mega-events. Interestingly, despite expressing a commitment to sport tourism as a driver of economic development, Northern Ireland has yet to develop any clear strategy to bid for or secure mega sport events. These arrangements pose questions about the political will, capacity, skills, and networks that home countries have to bid for and host mega events in their home nation and how they may reconcile such interests with the broader UK-wide mega event strategy. The current arrangements reveal the distinct and, at times, confusing arrangements for elite sport across home nations and the UK. For some sports (mainly the professionalised sports), there remains a core home nation focus. We see this in football, cricket, and rugby (although cricket has a combined England and Wales governing body and rugby has maintained a tradition of competing as part of the British Lions). For the sports that form part of the Commonwealth Games, each home nation sport council will work with NGBs to identity and develop talent and select teams to represent the home nation and compete at the Games. In many cases, these athletes are the same athletes that compete for Team GB at world championships and Olympic/Paralympic Games.

Elite sport success (i.e., winning medals) has undoubtedly become a political priority across the UK. Given the structural arrangements and composition of 'Team GB' being a combination of athletes from across the home nations, this is perhaps unsurprising. Despite success in recent years, however, it is clear that under-representation and inequalities exist in the composition of 'Team GB' – with Wales, Scotland, and NI still under-represented. Furthermore, this emphasis in elite sport success has also resulted in an increasingly targeted approach to funding across all home nations. Nowhere has this been more clearly articulated than UK Sport's 'No Compromise' approach to elite sport. This approach was developed largely in response to Team GB's embarrassing performance at the Atlanta 1996 Games. This 'No Compromise' approach emphasised operational efficiency and effectiveness, utilising data analytics to allocate funding to sports and athletes that were calculated to be the best medal-winning prospects, strongly influencing a change in elite sport culture across the UK, reinforcing the importance of winning medals at any cost.

The 'No Compromise' approach has undoubtedly driven a series of deeply problematic incidents in elite sport. The incidents have begun to receive governmental attention and policy action (Bostock et al., 2018). While not explicitly discussed in the home nation chapters, this attention and action can be seen in two distinct areas: First, in the efforts to investigate and address concerns about the culture of elite sport. Here, the *Duty of Care in Sport Review* conducted by Baroness Tanni Grey-Thompson highlighted multiple factors of change and core recommendations for the UK system. Furthermore, specific cases of athlete abuse have led to large-scale NGB reviews (e.g., Football Sexual Abuse Scandal, the *Whyte Review* of British Gymnastics, and the independent reviews of British Athletics and British Cycling). Second, UK Sport have worked with home nation sports councils to develop the good governance code to drive ongoing improvements in sport governance. These developments are notable examples of how key events can interact with actors/networks, and institutions, to bring a review of policy choice that can ultimately lead to policy change.

Community sport

Reports in all home nations suggest that while community sport policy has shifted back and forth between a concern for sport for sports sake or sport for good (Coalter, 2013), the most recent iterations of policy across all four countries pursue a normative line of argument about the power of sport to deliver an active, healthy nation as well as developing communities that are inclusive and resilient. Unsurprisingly, at the national level, community sport policy is led by the four home nation sports councils alongside the National Assembly or Parliament and in ostensible cooperation with the UK-wide DCMS.

There is also a notable variance how sport and physical activity participation data is collected and measured across the home nations at a national level. In England, Sport England collect data through the Active Lives Survey (ALS) on an annual basis and Children and Young People (CYP) surveys on a biannual basis, respectively. Both Scotland and Northern Ireland depend on general household surveys, such as the Scottish Household Survey (SHS) and the Continuous Household Survey (CHS), respectively – the former run by Ipsos MORI on behalf of the Scottish Government and the latter through the Northern Ireland Statistics and Research Agency (NISRA). Additionally,

Northern Ireland also utilises the Children's Sport Participation and Physical Activity (CSPPA) study to understand youth participation. Wales relies upon the Welsh Government's National Survey for Wales in order to track participation rates. The use of different methodological approaches, instruments, and measures between home nations makes it difficult to directly compare participation rates between countries. Nonetheless, what can be drawn from the home nation cases is the consistent theme of stubbornly low participation rates.

It is also evident that participation rates across the home nations have been adversely impacted by the recent COVID-19 pandemic. The impact of COVID-19 and lockdown measures specifically appears to be a central concern to all contemporary policies and strategies across home nations. Home nation chapters identified the impact and need for additional financial support packages. In England, for example, Sport England has identified the need to "recover and reinvent" one of five priority issues in its latest strategy, *Uniting the Movement* (Sport England, 2021) – a strategy that was itself drafted and published during the pandemic. This commitment resulted in a £195 million additional investment into the sport and physical activity sector and included the creation of a £15 million *Community Emergency Fund* and a £21.5 million *Return to Play Fund* to support organisations through the pandemic. The Scotland chapter perhaps most pertinently identified the extent of the challenges faced by sport organisations (e.g., loss of connection, cancellation of events, loss of sponsorship revenues, a reduction in tourism, cash flow difficulties, unpaid workforces) and individuals (e.g., isolation, loneliness, and mental health problems). Despite this, however, some authors were also optimistic that the COVID-19 pandemic could be utilised as an opportunity to promote a greater awareness of the role that sport and physical activity can play in alleviating physical and mental health problems and for sport organisations to develop a greater sense of resiliency and improve organisational capacity.

At the sub-regional level, there have been interesting developments across the four nations, largely motivated by the need for a strategic yet localised method of implementing community sport policy. England deviated from direct support of local authorities at the turn of the 21st century with the creation and funding of County Sport Partnerships (CSPs) – growing a total of 45 partnerships across the country. More recently, these CSPs have morphed into 42 Active Partnerships (APs), emphasising their broader focus on sport, physical activity, and well-being. These partnerships are unique and very different to the implementation infrastructure for community sport in other home nations. In Wales, the *Baker Review* has recommended a similar sub-regional model with four Community Sport Active Partnership's overlapping the Welsh Health Authorities which may, given time, develop into a regionalised based provision. In Scotland and Northern Ireland, the implementation of community sport policy is led by local government primarily for reasons of scale and efficiency. One potential explanation for this is that the size and population of these home countries do not demand an additional tier of administration. For example, the Greater Sport AP in Manchester covers 2.8 million people across ten urban local authority boundaries. This is larger in population than Northern Ireland and similar in population to Wales. Thus, geographical considerations are important in shaping sport policy infrastructure. Such decisions may also be influenced by values and beliefs about who is best placed to implement community sport policy. In England, the largely inefficient experience of investing in local authorities throughout the 1990s led to Sport England pursuing a new delivery system from 2000 onwards, with NGBs and CSPs being central parts of the system.

At the local delivery level, the home nation cases also emphasised the dramatic cuts in funding and infrastructure that have affected community sport. In particular, traditional local authority sport development units are largely considered a thing of the past. Additionally, other investments targeting social deprivation, ageing populations, and young people in swimming were removed as not "fit for purpose" (UKRCS, 2018, p. 6). Some authors also identified the potential for such impacts exacerbating the social, mental, and community impacts of COVID-19 pandemic. Consequently, these cuts in funding and provision lead to important questions about the real value of community sport and the extent to which – with greatly reduced funding and capacity – policy implementors may be able to achieve broader social outcomes.

Physical education and school sport

Physical education and school sport (PESS) has subtle but important nuances and differences across the four countries. While all home nations embrace the rhetoric of health and education through PESS, the precise detail of the policies differs. For England, PE and school sport policy was described a domain of policy neglect', with the authors stressing the increasingly squeezed and marginalised nature of PE and school sport policy (Harris, 2018; Mackintosh, 2014; Mackintosh & Liddle, 2015). Alongside this, policy had evolved to embrace an

Conclusion 119

overwhelmingly competitive curriculum and after school sport system. It was suggested that a distinctive feature of policy was the proliferation of external coaching companies post-2013 for £150 million per year allocating around £16,000 per year to individual primary schools. While this investment was doubled in 2017/2018 to £320 million per year, it has brought about a potentially challenging (unintended) consequence in subcontracting PE and school sport, triggering a form of privatisation of internal PESS out of the sector in private coaching businesses. In contrast, Wales and Northern Ireland have shaped their work in PESS with underpinning of physical activity guidelines and in more recent times with an underlying emphasis on physical literacy. The physical literacy movement across the four home nations arguably originates in the SNI physical literacy (2005) plan and LISPA model for planning (Delaney et al., 2008). With origins in this global movement over 15 years ago it also shows how different the organisational and strategic visions for PESS have been across the home nations. Wales has taken to a parallel shaping of physical literacy in its sport policies since 2014. At the time of writing, there was little evidence for any physical literacy policy work in either Scotland or England.

The positioning of PESS policy has not been a straightforward issue. In Scotland, it is firmly educational as far as a national and regional directive. But, in contrast, the English NCPE (2013) has sat loosely with a health leaning. In Wales, recent recommendations of a government review for PE to be a core subject that is supported by the National Assembly of Wales, but then not implemented. PE most recently in Wales has been a subject underpinned by health like England in 2023. After-school and 'school sport' adds another layer of complexity to the structure and deliverables of PESS policy. The previously mentioned PE premium in England is a considerable investment, but in arguably non-differentiated, variable size and variable degrees of need across primary schools. PESS in secondary schools is driven across a mixed economy of state-owned, private, and academy schools with differential PE department resources, sizes of team, and skill bases. Wales has its own long-standing 20-year Drago Sport extracurricular programme run and supported through local government, although this has faced resource challenges post austerity era. Northern Ireland's approach led through physical literacy has used pilots where Irish Football Association (FA) and Gaelic Athletic Association (GAA) have started using non-qualified teacher delivering community coaching in the curriculum. Likewise, this freedom to break down the binary nature of PE and community sport delivery has also seen the launch of extended schools targeting poverty-focused projects. All four home nations show an appetite for wider stakeholder partnerships outside the core school and traditional PE delivery. The policies, stakeholders, and routes to this process differ, but the intent to broadly reshape PESS is present. Impact is also questioned to differential degrees, and the autonomy with individual schools can operate in achieving such policy goals.

Whilst all countries argue for sport policy delivering health policy, well-being, and inclusion, PESS remains in a silo. There is little evidence to suggest that PESS policy is being used to drive any meaningful attempt for positive change in lifelong health and well-being outcomes. Some gains perhaps have been made in SNI case where long-standing physical literacy models, programmes, and campaigns have been embedded. In other countries, status quo remains the outcome of what has been termed in this study 'policy neglect'. Far closer attention is needed to harness the human, environmental, and cultural/educational tools that four national education systems offer in relation to sport and physical activity policy. There is no shortage of patches of infrastructure, policy ideas, and stakeholder collaboration to address in the short term over 20+ years. But, ultimately, statistics illustrate that specifically in relation to stubborn inequalities of age, gender, race, ethnicity, and social deprivation, little has been reshaped by PESS.

Sport development programmes and policies

In terms of sport development programmes and policies within each nation, all chapters indicated that there had been a recent general shift from sport for sport sake to towards an increasingly wider social agenda that promotes the benefits of sport, with many recent programmes/initiatives and policies generally reflecting this underlying belief. Wales specifically draws upon the example of Free Swimming as a government-led initiative that struggled with multiple, often contradictory objectives and implementation problems, which ultimately led to policy failure.

Closely linked to this has been a general shift away from direct provision of sport and leisure services to more targeted and localised approaches to public investment. Sport development provision across the UK appears to be increasingly targeted and localised, with some indication from cases that government agencies are moving from top-down to adopting an increasingly bottom-up approach to community sport provision. For example, Sport England has shifted from a generalised approach to funding community sport projects to allocating

£100 million to 12 local delivery pilots across targeted communities across England. These pilots were designed to break down the significant barriers to sport participation and address inequalities in sport and physical activity participation. As mentioned above, these examples suggest that the traditional, top-down delivery of sport and physical activity – commonly overseen and supported by NGBs – appears to be less prominent than they once were with nations appearing to invest directly in infrastructure within specific communities as opposed to national-level programming. It is also important to recognise that this shift in delivery has brought about an additional alternative set of challenges in terms of delivery that also now need to be considered.

As well as sport development programmes being localised, many countries also highlighted that recent programmes have becoming increasing targeted towards under-represented groups (e.g., Black, Asian, and Minority Ethnic (BAME), disability, women, and girls). In Wales, several recent initiatives (e.g., Calls for Action) have been targeted at 'hard-to-reach' populations, with the chapter stating that "women and individuals living with a disability, from a BAME background and/or living in poverty are now the focus of policy-makers and practitioners". In Northern Ireland, Sport Northern Ireland continues to focus on target groups around key issues such as women and girls, disability, and active ageing. The Northern Ireland chapter also explicitly identified the Everybody Active programme, a four-year, £6.2 million, National Lottery-funded initiative in 11 district councils across Northern Ireland, designed to increase participation in sport and physical activity across key life-course transitions. The England chapter directly quoted government's latest strategy, stating that "We [the DCMS] will distribute funding to focus on those people who tend not to take part in sport, including women and girls, disabled people, those in lower socio-economic groups and older people" (DCMS, 2015, p. 10). Collectively, this suggests a general reorientation of UK sport policy towards focusing on targeted groups.

Despite an increasingly localised approach to delivery, however, all cases suggested, either directly or indirectly, that local authority provision of sport development programming has declined over the past decade or so. This decline can, in part, be explained by the economic crisis in 2008 and the subsequent austerity measures implemented by home nation governments, but also the more recent economic turmoil due to the financial impact of COVID-19 pandemic and the recent war in Ukraine.

The aforementioned decline in local authority provision has also been closely paralleled with a growth of the voluntary or third sector in providing local provision. The England chapter, for example, highlighted the role of national charities such as StreetGames and Sported which have become an increasingly prominent service providers of, and conduits for, sport and physical activity provision within communities. We have also seen some evidence of an increasing role of community trusts within professional club settings which now deliver a wide variety of programmes as a form of community outreach but also to deliver a range of wider social objectives (Mackintosh, 2021).

Challenges to sport development

While the authors of the home nations chapters identified a number of challenges confronting sport in each nation, there were three clear themes that emerged in all nations relating to *inequality, complexity,* and *resources*. We also identified a fourth theme, *need for ongoing development of research and evidence*, within two of the four cases.

The first challenge common to all four home nations is the deep-rooted issue of inequality. The England chapter referred to equality as a 'wicked problem', one that has no solution per se, but rather resolutions that can help to lessen the impact of the problem. In following Wilkinson and Pickett's (2009) *The Spirit Level* thesis, the problem of access to sport cannot be effectively addressed until the growing gap income equality is reversed. For Wales, although inequality was not identified as a specific challenge, it is clear that poverty and social deprivation are high priorities on the political agenda and that sport-related policies remain focused on tackling social and economic inequalities. In Scotland, there remains an alarming divide in social class and regional inequality, which directly shapes who plays what sports, where, and when. Although the Equality Act should address such issues, it has been found to be inadequate in addressing access to sport. For Northern Ireland, the historic and present tensions between Protestant and Catholic communities present a very real challenge that adversely influences access to sport.

The complexity of structures and governance arrangements was also a recurrent theme throughout the home nation chapters. To some extent, this challenge can be seen to be a symptom of the UK/home nation structural arrangements insomuch as these arrangements require sporting structures that govern at the home nation level and at the UK level. The challenge is exacerbated by the range and nature of structures across the UK, the fact that some structures are specific to a particular sector (school, community, or elite sport – i.e., APs or local authorities), whereas others cut across all sectors (i.e.,

Conclusion 123

NGBs), and the system of coordination across agencies relies more on network governance than it does hierarchical, top-down governance. In more specific terms, Northern Ireland referred to complexity in the multi-layers of governance across the political environment and the diversity of funding sources that lay across multiple sources. The English and Scottish sporting landscapes were viewed to be complex largely due to the wide and varied range of entities spanning the local, regional, and national levels. For Wales, complexity lays not only in the fragmented and ambiguous sporting landscape but also in the tension that underpins these structures and networks, particularly between the sport and health sectors and between the Welsh Government and Sport Wales.

The England chapter illuminates resource-related challenges and the competition for finite resources between NGBs, Active Partnerships, and other key stakeholders. In Scotland, much work remains in terms of winning the political and economic argument for sport. Whilst sport may be a focus on increasing politicisation across Scottish political parties, current government spending on sport remains stubbornly when compared to other nations. Furthermore, any opportunity to argue for increased funding is hampered by Scotland not having a Minister for Sport nor any voice within the cabinet to argue for additional financial provision. The Wales chapter emphasised the problem of funding across the sport landscape for people, places, and infrastructure, and stated that funding for sport across Welsh local authorities has been squeezed to the point where they have disinvested from community assets and closed public sport and recreation facilities. In short, the Welsh chapter argues that there are simply insufficient resources to the effective delivery of sport policy. In Northern Ireland, financial constraints are considered significant with Sport NI managing on a budget of less than £30 million per year to deliver with funding required to be equally distributed to the achievement of community and elite sport outcomes.

The fourth and final challenge is linked to the need for ongoing development of research and evidence. This was explicitly identified within both the Scotland and Wales cases. The past two decades has seen a growth in the evidence base to support sport policy, and whilst the production of this text is reflective of this growth, there remain ongoing and new challenges. In Wales, sport policy research has attracted growing interest but remains relatively underdeveloped. Areas of policy research which might be of interest are the consideration of cross-sector partnerships, governance, innovation, community asset transfers, whole systems approaches, and sustainable changes in participation. In Scotland, there remains a need for the exploration of new methods and approaches, particularly in relation to social science, which can support and underpin evidence-based policy. The role of academics in exploring new approaches in which social innovation and local solutions can be evidenced could be important and contrasts with traditional top-down, government-led sport policy strategies in Wales.

Methodological reflections and future research directions

In reflecting upon our general methodological approach, we are acutely aware of the limitations of the present study. As Jowell (1998) reminds us, comparative analysis is both difficult and challenging and that anyone attempting to conduct a comparative study should be as enthusiastic about their limitations as they are about their findings. In following that tradition, it is important to recognise that our comparative analysis more accurately reflects a *contextual descriptive* type design (Landman & Carvalho, 2017), with an emphasis on providing an in-depth, intensive exploration of cases in each home nation. The strength of the *contextual descriptive* approach is that it provides a detailed account of the context in question to extract general themes. In this manner, we adopted a relatively low-order comparative approach compared to studies that test theory or seek more predictive capabilities (Landman & Carvalho, 2017). Nonetheless, given the relatively unexplored territory of sport and physical activity policy processes and practices across the four home nations, this study was a necessary precursor to formulate more complex and higher-order comparative studies in this area.

Another methodological consideration, which we briefly discussed within the introduction chapter and to which we now return is the generalisability of our findings and the extent to which it is possible to make claims beyond our home nation cases. Here we see two main generalisability issues. The first is the extent to which it is possible to extend the analysis of our case studies to make more general claims regarding sport policy across the UK. Another issue is the extent to which it is possible to generalise our analysis beyond the UK to other regions and/or countries. Regarding the former, we are conscious of specific methodological limitations of the case-based approach (Ragin, 2014) and our dependency on the analysis and interpretation of contributors to be able to identify and analyse all relevant factors (key variables, events, stakeholders, and policies) in order to make claims about sport policy across the UK. In relation to the latter, we are reminded of

Houlihan's (1997) remarks that sport policy researchers should be sensitive "to the dangers of transposing the policy experience of country to another uncritically and within qualification" (p. 4), and we also recognise that all countries are subject to and shaped by social, cultural, and political factors. With that said, we still believe that our findings can provide useful insights into the broad evolution of sport policy processes across other Western democracies.

We are also aware that using researchers who are embedded and experts within their sport policy context generated a richer insight into each of the home nation contexts than could be gathered in isolation. It is important, nonetheless, to recognise that each contributor (and therefore each home nation chapter) is likely to be influenced by the interests and background of the contributors, all of whom approach the writing of their chapters and their analytical process from their own experience with their own philosophical and methodological research backgrounds. It is partly for this reason that we chose to adopt a predetermined analytical framework and defined key terminology with contributors early in the research process. Nonetheless, we recognise the inherent methodological trade-offs that were made with regard to providing sufficient structure through the adoption of an analytical framework to enable comparison, whilst also providing sufficient flexibility and freedom for researchers to identify and discuss key elements that they considered to be important within their own home nation context. These are difficult choices and require trade-offs and compromises when attempting to conduct a comparative study of this kind.

It is also perhaps for the above reasons that we have been deliberately tentative and cautious about our findings and the extent to which it is possible to meaningfully identify explanatory factors regarding the similarity and differences that may or may not exist between home nations and by extension to make claims about the sport policy process across the UK. We also felt it was important to recognise the challenges that we faced with regard to our own philosophical differences amongst the researchers and even the editorial team. These differences ultimately made the making of comparisons more difficult. We did not overtly explore ideas around positionality in the study. Nonetheless, we attempted to overcome (or at least mitigate) this issue by explicitly articulating our methodological approach prior to conducting the study and the consistent use of an analytical framework, but again we felt these differences, if openly acknowledged and more formally recognised, perhaps would have enabled more opportunities for understanding the nature and complexities of the sport policy process across the UK. By engaging meaningfully with differing philosophical traditions, we may garner a deeper understanding of sport policy.

A final methodological reflection is our general reliance upon secondary data (namely policy and organisational documents and survey data, e.g., participation data and reports) and existing academic and grey-area literature. Again, we feel it is important to recognise these as social artefacts and a reflection and outcome of social interaction between actors within the policy process. It is for this reason we believe that they offer a valuable insight into policymaking both within and across the UK. Nonetheless, future studies could provide more insight into sport policymaking across the UK utilising first-hand (i.e., primary data) account to inform their analysis.

In turning to our study contributions and future directions of research specifically, as we have already intimated, we believe that this study offers an important first step in providing a comprehensive account of sport and physical activity policy and processes in each home nation within the UK. In doing so, we offer the first study of its kind to systematically identify the similarities and differences of sport policy, processes, and practices across the UK. As a result, we have laid an important and necessary foundation for others to develop more higher-order comparative studies. What can also be drawn from our general findings in this chapter specifically is that there is a need to further (re-)investigate several key themes including the impact of devolution on sport and physical activity policy. The forces of devolution are only likely to be more influential as the process of devolution continues to gather pace (e.g., more recent calls for IndyREF2 in Scotland). Our analysis also revealed systemic, asymmetrical power relations between (1) Westminster and the other home nation governments and (2) sports councils and governing agencies that warrant further empirical investigation. What are the implications of these power dynamics for sport policy and decision-making? What impact do these imbalanced relationships have on sport policy- and decision-making? These are important questions that have yet to be meaningfully examined within the sport policy and management literature. Our study also revealed the inherent need to better understand and document the sport policy processes within Scotland, Wales, and Northern Ireland specifically. A lack of research within this area is, in part, a reflection of the relatively small number of researchers within the sport policy field, but also we suggest due to the continued dominance of England-centric accounts of sport policy in the UK that need to be corrected or at least openly acknowledged. Finally, there is a need for more comparative studies that examine specific domains such as physical education and school sport and community sport and other specific issues such as governance, doping, and athlete welfare, for example. A final extension of this work is the need for more studies that conduct intra-country or intra-regional comparative designs within the sport policy and management domain. We believe these types of studies have merit but have yet to be embraced by sport policy and management researchers to date who have focused predominantly on more grandiose comparative projects to compare sporting nations (see Dowling et al., 2018, on this point). This previous preoccupation is perhaps understandable for many reasons, but intra- rather than inter-comparisons enable us to begin to identify and tease apart the inherent complexities that exist within a sporting nation and to better understand how contextual factors influence policy- and decision-making. In other words, we believe that intra-comparative studies have the potential to further reveal the proverbial 'black box' (Easton, 1965) of (sport) policymaking to better understand both how and why policy is made.

References

Bloyce, D., & Smith, A. (2010). *Sport Policy and Development. An Introduction.* Routledge.

Bostock, J., Crowther, P., Ridley-Duff, R., & Breese, R. (2018). No plan B: The Achilles heel of high performance sport management. *European Sport Management Quarterly, 18*(1), 25–46.

Cairney, P. (2019). *Understanding Public Policy: Theories and Issues.* Red Globe Press.

Coalter, F. (2013). *Game Plan* and *The Spirit Level*: The class ceiling and the limits of sports policy? *International Journal of Sport Policy and Politics, 5*(1), 3–19.

DCMS (2015). *Sporting Future: A New Strategy for an Active Nation.* DCMS.

Delaney, B., Donnelly, P., & News, J. (2008). *Improving Physical Literacy* (p. 593). Sport Northern Ireland.

Dowling, M. (2021). Uniting the movement? A critical commentary on Sport England's new strategy. *Managing Sport and Leisure.* Advanced online publication. https://doi.org/10.1080/23750472.2021.1942170

Dowling, M., Brown, P., Legg, D., & Grix, J. (2018). Deconstructing comparative sport policy analysis: Assumptions, challenges, and new directions. *International Journal of Sport Policy and Politics, 10*(4), 687–704.

Dowling, M., & Harris, S. (2021). *Comparing Sporting Nations: Theory and Method.* Meyer & Meyer Sport.

Easton, D. (1965). *A Systems Analysis of Political Life.* Wiley.

Harris, J. (2018). *The Case for Physical Education becoming a Core Subject in the National Curriculum.* Available at: http://www.afpe.org.uk/physical-education/wp-content/uploads/PE-Core-Subject-Paper-20-3-18.pdf (accessed 21 October 2019).

Houlihan, B. (1997). *Sport, Policy, and Politics: A Comparative Analysis*. Routledge.

Houlihan, B. (2000). Sporting excellence, schools and sports development: The politics of crowded policy spaces. *European Physical Education Review*, 6(2), 171–193.

Houlihan, B., & Lindsey, I. (2013). *Sport Policy in Britain*. Routledge.

Houlihan, B., & White, A. (2002). *The Politics of Sports Development: Development of Sport or Development through Sport?* Routledge.

Jowell, R. (1998). How comparative is comparative research? *American Behavioral Scientist*, 42(2), 168–177.

Landman, T., & Carvalho, E. (2017). *Issues and Methods in Comparative Politics* (4th edition). Routledge.

Marsh, D., Richards, D., & Smith, M. (2003). Unequal plurality: Towards an asymmetric power model of British politics. *Government and Opposition*, 38(3), 306–332.

Mackintosh, C. (2014) Dismantling the School Sport Partnership infrastructure: Findings from a survey of physical education and school sport practitioners, *Education 3–13: International Journal of Primary, Elementary and Early Years Education*, 42 (4), 432–449.

Mackintosh, C. (2021) *Foundations of Sport Development*. Routledge.

Mackintosh, C. and Liddle, J. (2015) PE and school sports development governance in England: Big Society, autonomy and decentralisation in new network relationships, *Education 3–13*, 43(6), 603–620.

Ragin, C. (2014). *The Comparative Method: Moving Beyond Qualitative and Quantitative Strategies* (2nd edition). University of California Press.

Rhodes, R. A. W. (1997). *Understanding Governance: Policy Networks, Governance, Reflexivity and Accountability*. Open University Press.

Sport England (2021). *Sport England: Uniting a Movement*. Sport England.

UKRCS (2018). *Free Swimming in Wales: A Review*. An independent report prepared for Sport Wales. https://democracy.npt.gov.uk/documents/s52972/Free%20Swimming%20Report%20Final.pdf (Accessed 22 August 2022).

Wilkinson, R. G., & Pickett, K. (2009). *The Spirit Level: Why More Equal Societies Almost Always Do Better*. Allen Lane.

Appendix 1
Sport policy Across the United Kingdom
A comparative analysis

Page 1: Participant information sheet: section A

Section A: the research project

1 Title of project
Sport policy across the United Kingdom: a comparative analysis

2 Purpose of study
To conduct an intra-country comparative analysis of sport and physical activity policies, processes and practices between the home nations (England, Northern Ireland, Scotland and Wales)

3 Who is the researcher? *(or researchers if more than one person).*
This pilot project is co-ordinated by Dr Mathew Dowling (Anglia Ruskin University), Dr Spencer Harris (University of Colorado), and Dr Christopher Mackintosh (Manchester Metropolitan University) (co-principal investigators) supported by research assistants (postgraduate students)

4 Why have I been asked to participate?
You have been invited to participate in this project due to your specific expertise and knowledge about the sporting landscape within your home nation.

5 How many people will be asked to participate?
An estimated 40-80 participants will take part in this pilot study.

6 Do I have to take part?
No, participation in this study is entirely voluntary. You can refuse to take part without giving a reason.

7 Has the study got ethical approval?

The study has ethical approval from the School of Psychology and Sport Sciences Research ethics panel (SREP) at Anglia Ruskin University.

8 Legislation relating to this study

This study complies with the Data Protection Act (2018) adheres to the university data protection policies and guidelines.

9 What will happen to the results of the study?

The results of this study will be used to inform a larger comparative study which will be written up as an edited book. The findings will also be presented at academic conferences.

Appendix 1: Sport policy Across the United Kingdom

Page 2: Participant information sheet: section B

1 What will I be asked to do?
Participants are required to access an online questionnaire (hosted by Jisc.ac.uk) via a link provided to complete a short questionnaire (20 questions). The questionnaire should take you approximately 8-12 minutes to complete. The questions focus on your experiences of the policies, processes, and practices surrounding the delivery and coordination of sport within your country and across the home nations of the United Kingdom.

2 In relation to this specific research project, we need to make you aware of the following:
Dr Mathew Dowling and Andie Riches (on behalf of ARU), are responsible for the personal data you give to us as data controller.

3 The following information (data) will be collected:
- Name/ Contact details
- Experiences
- Opinions

4 What will happen to your data?
All information collected from you during your participation in this research will be psuedoanonymised. This means that identifiable information, such as people's names, will be removed from the data and a code will be assigned using generic organisational (e.g. active partnership, national governing body of sport) and generic job titles (e.g. senior official, partnership manager). The data will, however, still be able to be linked together by the researcher (data controllers) should this be required.

All research data will remain in the European Economic Area (EEA) and will be held internally on a secure server with only the data controller in compliance with ARU data protection policies and with the GDPR and Data Protection Act (2018).

5 Will I be reimbursed travel expenses?
N/A – no travel is required to participate in this research project.

6 Will I receive any payment to take part in the research?
N/A – participants will not receive any payment or reimbursement

7 Are there any possible disadvantages or risks to taking part?
There are no possible additional disadvantages or risks associated with taking part in this study beyond those typically experienced in everyday life. Your agreement to participate in the study does not affect your legal rights.

8 What are the likely benefits of taking part?
There are no direct benefits for your taking part in the study, but it will enable us to generate a better understanding of sport policy across the United Kingdom. We will also share the headline findings of the study with all those who participate upon request.

9 Can I withdraw at any time, and how do I do this?
Participants can withdraw from the study at any time and without giving a reason. You can do this by emailing Dr Mathew Dowling (mathew.dowling@aru.ac.uk). You also do not have to answer any questionnaire or interview questions they do not wish to.

10 What will happen to my data?
Our general privacy notice explaining our use of your personal data for research purposes is available here:
https://www.anglia.ac.uk/privacy-and-cookies/research-participants
Please visit this link for information about how long we keep your data, how we keep your data secure, how you can exercise your rights over your data, and make a complaint over our use of your data.

11 Can I withdraw my data from the study?
The survey information collected from you will be anonymous. This means that I won't be able to remove your data, because I won't know which belongs to you. If you agree to participate and are asked to do a follow-up interview, this data will be pseudo-anonymised, meaning that I can only remove your data if you ask me before I anonymise it. After this, I won't know which is your data so will not be able to do this. I will be able to remove your data up to the point when I start to analyse it, which will be approximately 01/01/22.

12 Whether there are any special precautions you must take before, during or after taking part in the study
N/A

13 Will I pass onto anyone else what you have told me?
No information will be passed on to third party organisations.

Appendix 1: Sport policy Across the United Kingdom

14 Summary of research findings
A summary of the research findings will be sent to all participants upon request.

15 Contact details for complaints
If you have any issues with the study please contact Dr Mathew Dowling (Mathew.dowling@aru.ac.uk). You can also contact the Office of the Secretary and Clerk's office directly. Email address: complaints@aru.ac.uk. Postal address: Office of the Secretary and Clerk, Anglia Ruskin University, Bishop Hall Lane, Chelmsford, Essex, CM1 1SQ.

1 Please confirm you have read and understood the above information provided *Required*

☐ Yes
☐ No

Page 3: Participant consent form

Participant consent form

Title of the project: Sport Policy across the United Kingdom: A Comparative Analysis

Main investigator and contact details: Dr Mathew Dowling (Anglia Ruskin University, UK) (Mathew.dowling@aru.ac.uk)

Members of the research team: Dr Spencer Harris (University of Colorado, US), Dr Christopher Mackintosh (Manchester Metropolitan University, UK), Andie Riches (postgraduate student)

1. I agree to take part in the above research. I have read the Participant Information Sheet (14 June 2021, V1.0) for the study.
2. I understand what my role will be in this research, and all my questions have been answered to my satisfaction.
3. I understand that I am free to withdraw from the research at any time, without giving a reason.
4. I am free to ask any questions at any time before and during the study.
5. I understand what information will be collected from me for the study.
6. For the purposes of the Data Protection Act (2018), if this project requires me to produce personal data, I have read and understood how Anglia Ruskin University will process it.
7. I understand what will happen to the data collected from me for the research.
8. I understand that quotes from me may be used in the dissemination of the research through academic outlets.
9. I understand that the follow-up interview will be recorded (if applicable).
10. I have been informed how my data will be processed, how long it will be kept and when it will be destroyed.
11. I have been provided with a copy of this form and the Participant Information Sheet V1.0.

2 Please confirm you are willing to take part in the study *Required*

- Yes
- No

Page 4: Glossary of terms

Country – a nation with its own government, occupying a particular territory.
High performance/elite sport – the highest level of competition within a sport usually international competition and the Olympic/Paralympic Games
Home nations – refers to constituent countries of the United Kingdom (England, Scotland, Wales, and Northern Ireland).
Local government - the administration of a particular county or district
Nation(ally) – the region within a home nation (England, Scotland, Wales and Northern Ireland)
National government - the government, or political authority, that controls a nation
Participation – purposeful active participation in sports related physical activities performed during leisure-time
Physical Activity - any bodily movement produced by skeletal muscles that requires energy expenditure. Physical activity refers to all movement including during leisure time, for transport to get to and from places, or as part of a person's work (World Health Organisation, 2020).
Sport – institutionalised competitive activities that involve rigorous physical exertion or the use of relatively complex physical skills by participants motivated by internal and external rewards (Coakley, 2014)
Sport system – interconnected and interdependent group of individuals and organisations that work together (albeit to varying extents) and operate within a geo-political boundary to achieve particular sport or sport related outcomes such as developing community sport (participation), produce international sporting success (medals), or wider social objectives
Stakeholder – a person with an interest or concern and can either affect or be affected by an organisation
Strategy – a plan of action designed to achieve a long-term or overall aim
United Kingdom (UK) – a country that includes England, Scotland, Wales and Northern Ireland.

Appendix 1: Sport policy Across the United Kingdom

Page 5: General

3 Organisation name:
➕ More info

4 Home nation:

- England
- Scotland
- Wales
- Northern Ireland

5 How would you describe the sport and physical activity system within your home nation?

6 Who do you consider to be the key stakeholders responsible for delivering sport *participation* and physical activity objectives within your home nation?

7 Who do you consider to be the key stakeholders responsible for delivering *high performance sport* objectives within your home nation?

138 Appendix 1: Sport policy Across the United Kingdom

Page 6: Roles and responsibilities/issues

8 Please indicate the extent to which you agree or disagree with the following statements:

Please don't select more than 1 answer(s) per row.

	Strongly agree	Agree	Neither agree or disagree	Disagree	Strong Disagree
Roles and responsibilities of key stakeholders within sport and physical activity are clearly defined	⌐	⌐	⌐	⌐	⌐
Your sporting system operates independently from other home nations	⌐	⌐	⌐	⌐	⌐
Your home nations sporting landscape as a co-ordinated system	⌐	⌐	⌐	⌐	⌐
The home nations have a co-ordinated sport and physical activity system	⌐	⌐	⌐	⌐	⌐
Co-ordination could be improved in relation to the planning and delivery of sport and physical activity within your home nation	⌐	⌐	⌐	⌐	⌐
Co-ordination could be improved in relation to the planning and delivery of sport and physical activity across the UK	⌐	⌐	⌐	⌐	⌐

Appendix 1: Sport policy Across the United Kingdom

	Strongly agree	Agree	Neither agree or disagree	Disagree	Strong Disagree
Communication could be improved in relation to the planning and delivery of sport and physical activity within your home nation	☐	☐	☐	☐	☐
Communication could be improved in relation to the planning and delivery of sport and physical activity across the UK	☐	☐	☐	☐	☐
Historically sport and physical activity policy across the UK has been England-centric	☐	☐	☐	☐	☐
Current sport and physical activity policy across the UK is England-centric	☐	☐	☐	☐	☐
Sport and physical activity is a priority for local governments in your country	☐	☐	☐	☐	☐
Sport and physical activity is a national government priority in your country	☐	☐	☐	☐	☐
Austerity measures have affected your ability to deliver your objectives	☐	☐	☐	☐	☐

140 Appendix 1: Sport policy Across the United Kingdom

	Strongly agree	Agree	Neither agree or disagree	Disagree	Strong Disagree
Austerity has impacted your capabilities as an organisation	☐	☐	☐	☐	☐
COVID-19 has affected your ability to deliver your objectives	☐	☐	☐	☐	☐
Your home nation will become independent (i.e., devolution) in the next 5 years	☐	☐	☐	☐	☐
Your home nation will become independent (i.e., devolution) at some point in the future	☐	☐	☐	☐	☐
Devolution would impact how you operate as an organisation	☐	☐	☐	☐	☐

9 Any additional comments regarding roles and responsibilities and issues within your home nation or the United Kingdom?

Page 7: Funding and support

10 Please indicate whether you agree or disagree with the following statements:

Please don't select more than 1 answer(s) per row.

	Strongly agree	Agree	Neither agree or disagree	Disagree	Strong Disagree
There is sufficient funding for high performance sport within your home nation	▢	▢	▢	▢	▢
There is sufficient funding for high performance sport across the UK	▢	▢	▢	▢	▢
There is sufficient funding for improving sport participation levels within your home nation	▢	▢	▢	▢	▢
There is sufficient funding for improving sport participation levels across the UK	▢	▢	▢	▢	▢
Sports are given equal funding and support within your home nation	▢	▢	▢	▢	▢
Sports should be given equal funding and support across the UK	▢	▢	▢	▢	▢
High performance sport is given priority within your home nation	▢	▢	▢	▢	▢

Appendix 1: Sport policy Across the United Kingdom

High performance sport should be given priority within the UK	☐	☐	☐	☐	☐
Sport participation and physical activity is given priority within your home nation	☐	☐	☐	☐	☐
Sport participation and physical activity should be given priority within the UK	☐	☐	☐	☐	☐
Your national governing agency for sport and physical activity is effective at supporting high performance athletes	☐	☐	☐	☐	☐
Your national governing agency for sport and physical activity is effective at supporting sport participation	☐	☐	☐	☐	☐

11 Any additional comments regarding funding and support within your home nation or the United Kingdom?

```
                                                      
                                                      
                                                      
```

Page 8: Leadership and strategy

12 Please indicate the extent to which you agree or disagree with the following statements:

Please don't select more than 1 answer(s) per row.

	Strongly agree	Agree	Neither agree or disagree	Disagree	Strong Disagree
Sport is governed effectively within your home nation	☐	☐	☐	☐	☐
Sport is governed effectively across the UK	☐	☐	☐	☐	☐
There is a strong degree of diversity in the leadership of sport and physical activity within your home nation	☐	☐	☐	☐	☐
There is a strong degree of diversity in the leadership of sport and physical activity within the UK	☐	☐	☐	☐	☐
I support the current strategy for sport and physical activity within my home nation	☐	☐	☐	☐	☐
I supported the previous strategy for sport and physical activity within my home nation	☐	☐	☐	☐	☐
Your organisations' voice was heard during the consultation of this strategy	☐	☐	☐	☐	☐

Appendix 1: Sport policy Across the United Kingdom

13 Any additional comments regarding current or previous strategy for developing sport and physical activity within your home nation or across the UK?

Appendix 1: Sport policy Across the United Kingdom

Page 9: Any other comments

14 Please use the space below to discuss anything else you feel has not been addressed above that you think is important to understanding sport policy and physical activity within your home nation or across the UK

15 Would you be willing to take part in a short follow-up interview?

- Yes
- No

16 If yes, please provide an appropriate email address

Page 10: Final page

Thank you for taking part in this survey

Appendix 2

Sport Policy Across the United Kingdom (SPATUK) – Systematic Review[1]

Search parameters: peer-reviewed journal articles and books, English, 1990–present (December 2021)

Databases: SportDiscus, Scopus, ProQuest (Sociology), ProQuest (Sport Science)

Search terms: (sport policy OR sport development OR sport landscape OR sport system OR sport organisation) AND (home nation OR Great Britain OR United Kingdom OR England OR English OR Scotland OR Scottish OR Wales OR Welsh OR Northern Ireland OR Northern Irish)

Inclusion/exclusion – applied post-hoc

- Full-text journal article or book
- Must predominantly focus on sport development/policy/management or sport history
- Must focus on one or more home nation countries (England, Scotland, Wales, and Northern Ireland)

PRISMA flowchart:

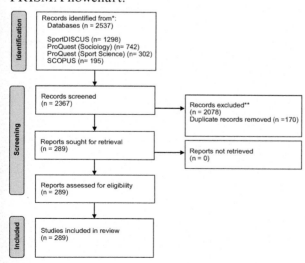

Note

1 We would like to formally acknowledge the contribution of Andie Riches, a postgraduate student at Anglia Ruskin University for her help and support with conducting this systematic review and pilot survey on behalf of the editors.

Index

Note: **Bold** page numbers refer to tables and *italic* page numbers refer to figures.

Action Sport programmes 31–32
active fit/sporty 103
Active Lives Survey (ALS) 23, 116
active living, no limits 102–103
Active Living Strategy 89, 95, 100, 104
active partnerships (AP) 21, 28, 35, 117
Active People Survey (APS) 23
Active School Travel programme 101
Active Young People Programmes (AYPP) 71, *72*
adequate provision 49–50
all-encompassing strategy 62
analytical framework 14, **15**, 125
aspirations 29, 35, 55
asymmetrical power relations 126

Belfast Agreement 83, 86, 87
Big Society 32
black, Asian and minority ethnic (BAME) 24, 74–75, 121
bonfire of the quangos 63
British cultural identity 103
British political system 110
budgetary constraint 54
business-oriented practices 33

case-based approach 11–13
case-based research design 10
case-oriented approach 11
Central Council of Physical Recreation (CCPR) 21

Children and Young People (CYP) 116
Children's Sport Participation and Physical Activity (CSPPA) 96, 99, 117
children/young people 96–98
civil society activism 32
collaborative dissonance 69–70
commercialisation 6
Commonwealth Games 2, 48, 56, 67, 68, 77, 83, 113, 115
Community Amateur Sports Club Scheme 42
community sport 116–118
community sport participation 27, 97, **97**
comparativist approach 11
conservative-led governments 29, 30
context specific policy 61–62
contextual descriptive approach 124
Continuous Household Survey (CHS) 91, 94, 116
Convention of Scottish Local Authorities (COSLA) 51
cost-of-living crisis 50
County Sport Partnerships (CSPs) 21, 23, 117 (see also Active Partnerships)
crowded policy space 112
cultural heritage 60
cultural heterogeneity 13
cultural property 41
culture/recreation services 56

150 *Index*

Curriculum, Examinations and Assessment (CCEA) 98
Curriculum Sports Programme 100–101

Daily Mile 101
data collection technique 10
DCMS *see* Department of Digital, Culture, Media and Sport (DCMS)
Department for Communities (DfC) 87
Department for Economy (DfE) 90–91
Department for Education (DE) 90, 99
Department of National Heritage (DNH) 22
devolution 3–6, 62, 65–67, 76, 77, 109–110
Department of Digital, Culture, Media and Sport (DCMS) 6–7, 20, 34, 35, 45, 112

economic development 65, 115
economic/social reforms 4
economic viability 91
educational attainment 94
elite-level athletes 25
elite sport: England 24–26; national culture and identity 115; no compromise approach 116; Northern Ireland 91–94; political priority 115; Scotland 47–49; talent identification and development 114; under-representation and inequalities 115; Wales 66–68
elite sport development systems 24–26
embedded case study design 12, *12*
embedded, multi-case design 10
England-centric approach 9, 10, 12
English Institute of Sport (EIS) 21, 25
English laws system 4
English policy dominance 110–112
English Sports Council 22
European Economic Area (EEA) 131
Every Body Active 102
evidence-based policy 77, 124

evolution of sport policy: convergence and change 113–114; devolution 109–110; jurisdictional overlap and stakeholder involvement 112–113; Westminster/English policy dominance 110–112
exchequer funding 88
exogenous influences 2, 5
experimental/statistical methods 10
extended schools programme 101–102
external funding 32
extracurricular sport policy development 73–74

financial constraints 103, 123
financial investment 92
financial resources 76
flagship programmes 73
flip-flopping 76
Football Association (FA) 119
foundation blocks 95, *95*
fragmentation 33, 35, 69
functional equivalence 108
funding support 141–142

Gaelic Athletic Association (GAA) 101, 119
Game Plan 23
gender imbalance 49
generalisability 13, 124
genuinely cross-government approach 34
globalisation 6
Governance and Leadership Framework for Wales (GLFW) 68
governmentalisation 6
grassroots delivery agents 87
Great Britain and Northern Ireland (GB&NI) 67

hard-to-reach communities 76
Hargreaves, J. 32
Harris, J. 30
Harris, S. 7, 129, 134
Hayton, J.W. 33
Healthy and Active Fund (HAF) 75
Higher Education Institutions (HEIs) 75

Index

Hollingsworth, T. 24
Holyrood Parliament 44, 47
home championships 68
human rights 46

independence 3–6
inequality gap 54
international sporting competition 2, 6
intra-country comparative analysis 2, 10
intra-country/intra-regional comparative designs 127
Irish Football Association (IFA) 101

joined-up thinking 23
jurisdictional overlap 112–113

labour's dominance 76
Labour's School Sport Partnerships system 30
leadership 143–144
legislative requirements 53
life-course transitions 121
Lifelong Involvement in Sport and Physical Activity (LISPA) 99–100
local authorities (LAs) 21, 28, 54, 61, 69
local delivery models 56
Local Government Act 89
localised/place-based approaches 28
localities 40, 57 n1
marketisation 61, 110
mass-elite dilemma 114
mass participation 22
MDSD *see* most different system design (MDSD)
Members of the Scottish Parliament (MSPs) 44
methodological reflection 124–127
mission drift 33
modernising 20
Monarchy of the United Kingdom 44
money criteria 104
most different system design (MDSD) 11
most similar systems design (MSSD) 11, 12
multi-culturalism 4

National Assembly 6
National Assembly for Wales 73
national charities 122
National Curriculum for Physical Education (NCPE) 29
national education systems 120
National Governing Bodies of Sport (NGBs) 21, 35, 36, 61, 109
nationalism 4
national-level organisations 9
national-level programming 121
National Lottery funding 67, 88
national organisations 61
national population health strategies 43
National Records of Scotland (NRS) 40, 57 n1
national sporting contests 2
national stakeholders 27
natural resources 5
Natural Resources Wales (NRW) 61, 109
New Statistical Account 41
non-departmental public body (NDPB) 20, 99
non-profit organisations 31
non-sport-focused organisations 104
non-sporting outcomes 56
non-statutory service 35, 76
Northern Ireland Statistics and Research Agency (NISRA) 116

organisational system 30
outcomes-based accountability 88
outcomes-based framework 88
outdoor sports 43, 52

parity of esteem principle 83, 86, 104
participant consent form 134
participant information sheet 131–133
participation/community sport: England 26–29; Northern Ireland 94–98; Scotland 49–51; Wales 68–70
Peace Dividend 86
performance-led sporting infrastructure 67
performance pathway models 25

152   Index

physical education (PE) 53, 73, 99
physical education and school
   sport (PESS): England 29–31;
   home nations 118; Northern
   Ireland 98–102; positioning 119;
   private coaching businesses 119;
   privatisation 119; Scotland 51–53;
   Wales 70–74
physical literacy 99–100
Physical Literacy Programme for
   Schools (PLPS) 71
policy development 1, 14, 23, 71
policy domains 77
policy environment 2
policymaking process 14, 113
policy neglect 120
policy shifts 113–114
policy transition 88
political economy 55
politicisation 123
politico-religious markers 86
population-level evaluation
   model 104
poverty 62, 122
presentation specific policy 62
primary schools 30, 31
privatisation 61, 110, 119
professional sports 60
Programme for Government (PfG) 87
project-level outcomes 104
Public Health Wales (PHW) 61, 109
public investment 120
public leisure intervention 70

quantitative-based monitoring
   criteria 104

regional differences 13
regionalisation 70
Regional Sport Partnerships 75
Republic of Ireland (ROI) 83, *84*
rights-based approach 53

school-based physical activity
   participation 53
school estate 51–52
Scottish football's financial
   dependency 41
Scottish Government 41–42
Scottish Household Survey
   (SHS) 116

Scottish Institute of Sport (SIS) 115
Scottish National Party (SNP) 5, 45
Scottish sporting ecosystem 42
secondary schools 30
segregation 86
self-esteem 94
self-governing entities 85
self-selecting process 11
settlements 40, 57 n1
singular analytical framework 10
'small-N' approach 11
social cohesion 51
social deprivation 62, 118, 122
social inequality 51
social issues 22
social welfare programme 1
socio-economic deprivation 69, 71
socioeconomic influences 24
sport development: challenges
   122–124; challenges and barriers
   75–77, 103–104; Northern Ireland
   102–104; programmes and policies
   120–122; Wales 74–77
sport development programmes and
   policies 102–103
sport-for-development
   organisations 33
sporting structures 6
Sport Northern Ireland (SNI) 84
Sport Northern Ireland Sports
   Institute (SNISI) 84, 115
sport/physical activity continuum *90*
sport policy: comparative analysis
   3; goals 2; home nations 1; school
   and community 6
Sport policy across the United
   Kingdom (SPATUK) 147–148
springboard effect 92
stakeholder involvement 112–113
Statistical Account of Scotland 41
statutory responsibility 104
Sugar Tax 30
sustainability 33
sustainable development goals
   (SDGs) 46, 51, 54, 56

talent identification 25, 92,
   93, 94
target-driven culture 77
tax reliefs 42
teaching professionals 31

transport capital budget 46
troubles 83, 86
two-tier system 61
UK National Lottery system 42
UK Sports Council 22
unemployment 32, 83
unification 3–6
United Kingdom of Great Britain 2, 3, 145
United Nations Convention on the Rights of the Child (UNCRC) 53
United States of America (USA) 41
universalism 32
urban communities 31

vision 65, 69

Well-Being of Future Generations (Wales) Act 2015 (WBFGA) 66, **66**, 75, 77
Welsh devolution 62
Welsh Institute of Sport (WIS) 115
Westminster 12, 40, 110–112
Whole Sport Plans (WSPs) 23
wicked problem 23, 24, 36, 122
Wolfenden Report 21
world class 47–48
World Health Organisation 70
young people's participation 71

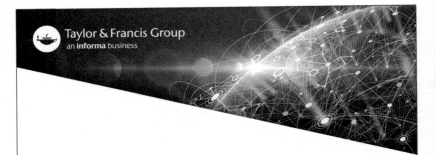